712-7T

# teach®
# yourself

## excel 2003

moira stephen

# teach® yourself

## excel 2003

moira stephen

for over 60 years, more than 40 million people have learnt over 750 subjects the **teach yourself** way, with impressive results.

be where you want to be with **teach yourself**

For UK orders: please contact Bookpoint Ltd, 130 Milton Park, Abingdon, Oxon OX14 4SB. Telephone: +44 (0) 1235 827720. Fax: +44 (0) 1235 400454. Lines are open 09.00-18.00, Monday to Saturday, with a 24-hour message answering service. Details about our titles and how to order are available at www.teachyourself.co.uk.

For USA order enquiries: please contact McGraw-Hill Customer Services, PO Box 545, Blacklick, OH 43004-0545, USA. Telephone: 1-800-722-4726. Fax: 1-614-755-5645.

For Canada order enquiries: please contact McGraw-Hill Ryerson Ltd., 300 Water St, Whitby, Ontario L1N 9B6, Canada. Telephone: 905 430 5000. Fax: 905 430 5020.

Long renowned as the authoritative source for self-guided learning – with more than 30 million copies sold worldwide – the *Teach Yourself* series includes over 300 titles in the fields of languages, crafts, hobbies, business, computing and education.

*British Library Cataloguing in Publication Data*

A catalogue record for this title is available from The British Library.

*Library of Congress Catalog Card Number:* On file.

First published in UK 2004 by Hodder Headline, 338 Euston Road, London NW1 3BH.

First published in US 2004 by Contemporary Books, A Division of the McGraw-Hill Companies, 1 Prudential Plaza, 130 East Randolph Street, Chicago, Illinois 60601 USA.

The 'Teach Yourself' name is a registered trade mark of Hodder & Stoughton Ltd.

🕮 Typeset by MacDesign, Southampton

Printed in Great Britain for Hodder & Stoughton Educational, a division of Hodder Headline, 338 Euston Road, London NW1 3BH by Cox & Wyman Ltd, Reading, Berkshire.

Papers used in this book are natural, renewable and recyclable products. They are made from wood grown in sustainable forests. the logging and manufacturing processes conform to the environmental regulations of the country of origin.

Impression number   10  9  8  7  6  5  4  3  2  1
Year                 2007  2006  2005  2004

**contents**

Welcome to **Teach Yourself Excel**.

If you need to produce budgets, forecasts, summary data, statistics, financial information, charts, lists of data and interactive spreadsheets you'll find all the features you require in Excel.

This book will help you unleash the power of Excel, quickly and painlessly. We start by introducing the basic skills that are needed to create and format a workbook attractively. Simple formulas and sophisticated formatting options will help ensure that your worksheets are not only accurate, but look good too!

We then move on to introduce the many different and powerful functions that are available in Excel. Logical, statistical, math, text, date, financial and lookup functions are all discussed.

Other features covered include charting and drawing, styles and templates, list management, macros, integration of Excel with the other applications in the Office suite, using Excel to e-mail and preparing Web pages in Excel.

Excel is a very powerful spreadsheet package – but don't let that put you off – you'll be amazed at what can be achieved easily!

I hope you enjoy using this book and find it useful when learning to use Excel.

**Moira Stephen**
**2004**

# 01

# getting started

**In this chapter you will learn:**

- what you need to run Excel 2003
- how to install the software
- how to start Excel
- about the Excel screen and its tools
- how to use the Help system

## Aims of this chapter

This chapter introduces the spreadsheet package **Excel**. We will start with an overview of the package, and consider the hardware and software specifications required to run **Excel** successfully. We then move on to look at how you install the package on your computer. Getting into **Excel**, the working environment, online **Help** system and exiting **Excel** will also be discussed.

# 1.1 Introducing Excel

Excel is a very powerful spreadsheet package – but don't let that put you off! You can use Excel to produce simple spreadsheets to help you prepare your invoices, budgets and summary statements. You can also use Excel to chart your data, manipulate it using database-type features and publish your worksheet to the Web. Excel integrates well with the other packages in Microsoft Office and you'll find out how you can use this to your advantage. Finally, Excel is very Web orientated – you'll soon be able to hyperlink to other files and Internet addresses, send e-mails and publish your worksheets and charts on the Web.

It is assumed that you have a working knowledge of Windows.

# 1.2 Hardware and software requirements

The hardware and software specifications given are for Office 2003.

The recommended configuration is a PC with a minimum of a Pentium III Processor and 128 MB of RAM.

The minimum specification is given in the table opposite.

See **http://www.microsoft.com/uk/office/sysreq.asp** for full details of system requirements.

| Processor | 133 MHz or higher; Pentium III recommended |
|---|---|
| Operating system | Windows 2000 with Service Pack 3, Windows XP, or a later system |
| RAM | 64 MB (128 MB recommended) for the operating system, plus 8 MB for each program running simultaneously |
| Hard disk | Approximately 245 MB in total, with 115 MB on the hard disk where the operating system is installed. |
| CD-ROM drive | |
| Monitor | Super VGA or higher resolution |
| Mouse | Microsoft Mouse, IntelliMouse® or compatible pointing device |

# 1.3 Installing Excel

Excel is supplied in all the Office suite editions. For full details of what is included in each edition visit **http://www.microsoft.com/uk/office/editions.asp**

**To install Microsoft Office, follow the on-screen instructions:**

**1** Insert the CD into the CD drive.

◆ The CD will launch automatically, and the setup begin.

**2** At the **Setup** dialog box, enter the 25-character product key.

**3** For the user information, enter your name, initials (optional) and organization (optional).

◆ Your name will be used in the Author box in the Properties dialog box in the Office programs.

**4** Read the End-User License Agreement and select *I* **accept the terms** ... (If you don't agree, you can't continue!).

**5** Select the type of installation.

**6** At the final Setup stage, select the options and you're done!

## Activate your software

The first time that you open an Office application you will be prompted to activate your software. If you don't activate it, you can open the applications a total of 50 times, then many of the features become inactive. Activation verifies the legitimacy of your licence and discourages software piracy. It's very easy to do – just follow the prompts and activate it online – it takes 2 seconds!

## 1.4 Starting Excel

1 Click the **Start** button on the Taskbar.

2 Point to **All Programs**.

3 Select **Microsoft Office**.

4 Click **Microsoft Office Excel 2003**.

# 1.5 The Excel screen

When Excel starts, you are presented with a new workbook displaying a blank worksheet. We'll take a tour of the Excel screen, so that you know what the various areas are called.

If the Workbook window is maximized, the Workbook and the Application windows share one Title bar containing the Application and Workbook names.

You'll find the different screen areas referred to by the names given below in the online Help and throughout this book.

Application Title bar

Application Minimize, Maximize/
Restore and Close buttons

Menu bar

Formatting toolbar

Standard toolbar

Ask a question box

Formula bar

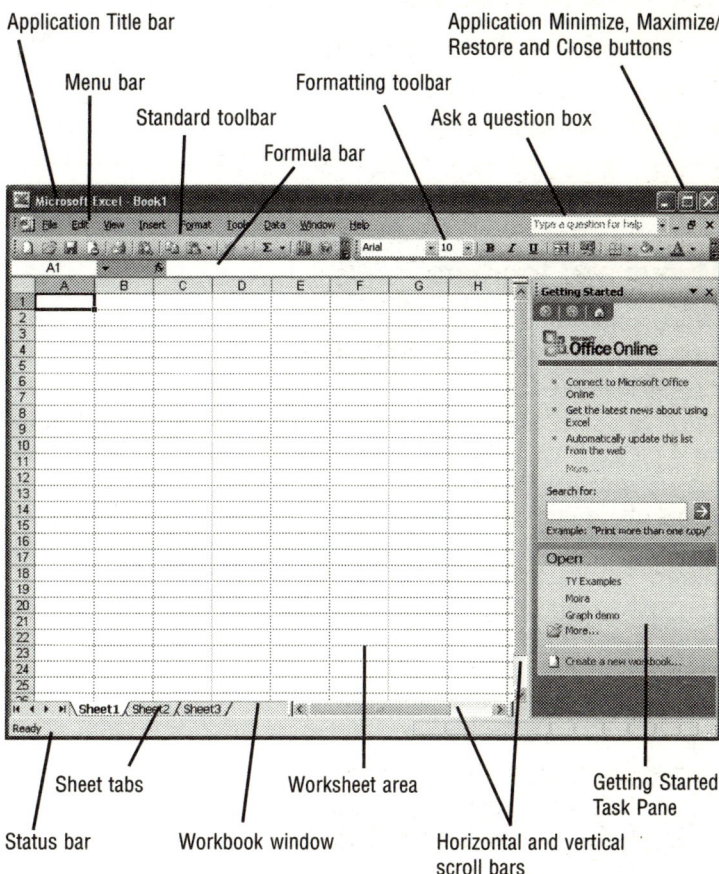

Sheet tabs

Worksheet area

Getting Started
Task Pane

Status bar

Workbook window

Horizontal and vertical
scroll bars

# 1.6 Workbooks and worksheets

When working in Excel, the files that you create and work with are called workbooks, each consisting of a number of worksheets. A worksheet is the primary document, and consists of cells organized in rows and columns. The default number of worksheets in a workbook is three, but you can add more if necessary, or remove any that you don't need.

Related data is usually best kept on separate worksheets within the same workbook – this makes it easier to find and manage your data.

For example, if you were collating regional sales figures, you could record the figures for each region on a separate sheet within the same workbook. Alternatively, you could have a separate workbook for each region and record the monthly or quarterly sales figures on separate sheets within each region's workbook.

Worksheets will be discussed more fully in Chapter 4.

## Menus and toolbars

Office applications personalize your menus and toolbars automatically. The items that you use most often are featured on your personalized toolbars or menus.

Once you start using Excel, you'll find that the menu options most recently used will be displayed first when you open a menu (this is your personalized menu). You can expand the menus to reveal all commands (simply click on the down arrow that appears at the bottom of each menu). You may find that the menu automatically expands if you just wait once you've opened it. If you wish to modify the way that the menus work, open the View menu choose Toolbars, Customize. You can switch the **Always show full menus** or *Show* **full menus after a short delay** options on or off on the Options tab.

The Standard and Formatting toolbars share a single row, so that you have more room for your work (if you wish to disable the row sharing option see Chapter 11). Click the drop-down arrow to the right of a toolbar to display additional tools. The tools that you used most recently are displayed on the visible part of the toolbar on your screen.

See Chapter 11 for more information on toolbars.

*Don't panic if your toolbars and menus are not exactly the same as those illustrated in this book.*

## Task Pane

The **Getting Started** Task Pane appears on the right side of the screen each time that you start Excel. You can easily close the Task Pane by clicking the Close button at the top right of it.

You will use a number of Task Panes when working in Excel. The **Clipboard** Task Pane can be used when copying and moving items (see section 2.13) and the **Styles and Formatting** and **Reveal Formatting** Task Panes are useful when formatting documents (see Chapter 3).

You can display any Task Pane by selecting it from the Task Pane list.

Getting Started ▾ ×
- ✓ Getting Started
- Help
- Search Results
- Clip Art
- Research
- Clipboard
- New Workbook
- Template Help
- Shared Workspace
- Document Updates
- XML Source

**Open**
- TY Examples
- Moira
- Graph demo
- More...

Create a new workbook...

## Smart tags

As you work with Excel you will notice that 'smart tags' appear at various times, e.g. when you copy and paste some data (see section 2.13). If you click the smart tag it will display a list of options that allow you to control or customize the task that you are performing.

# 1.7 Menus

There are nine main menus in the Excel Window. You can use these to access any function or feature in Excel. I suggest that you have a browse through them to get an idea of what's available – some menu items may be familiar to you, some will be new. You can display a menu and select menu options, just as in any Windows application, using either the mouse or the keyboard.

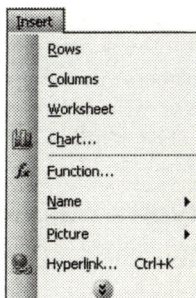

Insert
- Rows
- Columns
- Worksheet
- Chart...
- Function...
- Name ▸
- Picture ▸
- Hyperlink... Ctrl+K

**To open and select from menus using the mouse:**

1  Click on the menu name to display the list of options available in that menu.

2  Click on the menu item you wish to use.

•  Click the extension arrow at the bottom of your personalized menu to display all the options available.

**To open a menu using the keyboard:**

•  Hold down [**Alt**] and press the underlined letter, e.g. to open the File menu press [**Alt**]-[**F**] to open the Insert menu press [**Alt**]-[**I**].

Each item in a menu also has a letter underlined in it.

**To select an item from the menu using the keyboard:**

•  Press the underlined letter.

Or

•  Use the up and down arrow keys until the item you want is selected, then press [**Enter**].

Once a menu is displayed, you can press the right or left arrow keys to move from one menu to another.

**To close a menu without selecting an item from the list:**

•  Click the menu name again, click anywhere off the menu or press [**Esc**].

In addition to the menus, many of the commands can be initiated using the toolbars, keyboard shortcuts or shortcut menus. Each of these will be covered as you progress through the book.

# 1.8 Help!

As you work with Excel you will most probably find that you come a bit unstuck from time to time and need help. There are several ways of getting Help – most of them very intuitive and user-friendly.

## Type a question for help box

You can access the Help system using the Type a question for help box on the menu bar.

1 Type in your question.

how do I insert a row

2 Press [Enter].

3 Choose the Help topic required from the Search Results Task Pane that is displayed – click on it.

**Search Results**

For additional and updated content, search Microsoft Office Online.
Learn more

20 results

- Insert blank cells, rows, or columns
- Turn on or off Insert Options
- Specify how new data is added to an external data range
- Print a PivotTable report
- Add or delete rows or columns to a list
- Add, delete, or move page breaks

**Search**

Offline Help

how do I insert a row

Can't find it?

## Excel Help Task Pane

To show the Excel Help Task Pane:

◆ Click the **Excel Help** tool on the Standard toolbar.

Or

◆ Press [**F1**].

The Task Pane has three main areas:

◆ The Offline Help can be accessed from the **Search for:** field and the **Table of Contents** option at the top.

◆ The Online Help can be accessed from the middle area.

◆ Topics like 'What's New', 'Contact Us' and 'Accessibility Help' can be accessed from the **See also** list at the bottom of the Task Pane.

The icons at the top of a Task Pane take you Back or Forwards through the topics that you have used recently, or Home to the Getting Started Task Pane.

**Excel Help**

**Assistance**

Search for:

Table of Contents

**Office Online**

- Connect to Microsoft Office Online
- Get the latest news about using Excel
- Automatically update this list from the web
- More...

- Assistance
- Training
- Communities
- Downloads

**See also**

- What's New
- Contact Us
- Accessibility Help
- Online Content Settings...

0000000000000000000000000000000

## Search for

1 Enter a keyword or keywords in the **Search for:** field at the top of the Excel Help Task Pane.

2 Press [**Enter**] or ⬛ to display a list of topics on the subject.

3 Click on the topic that sounds most likely in the Search Results Task Pane to display the Help page.

If you can't find the Help that you need, click *Can't find it?* at the bottom of the Search Results Task Pane – Excel will suggest how you could make your search more successful.

You can also search another location in the **Search** options at the bottom of the Task Pane, or try different keywords.

## Table of Contents

You can browse through the Help with this option.

1 Click ⬛ Table of Contents near the top of the Task Pane.

2 Click on a book in the Table of Contents list – the book will open to display other books or the titles of topics.

* You can adjust the width of the Table of Contents pane by dragging the left edge of it.

3 Open another book, or click on a topic to display the Help page on that topic.

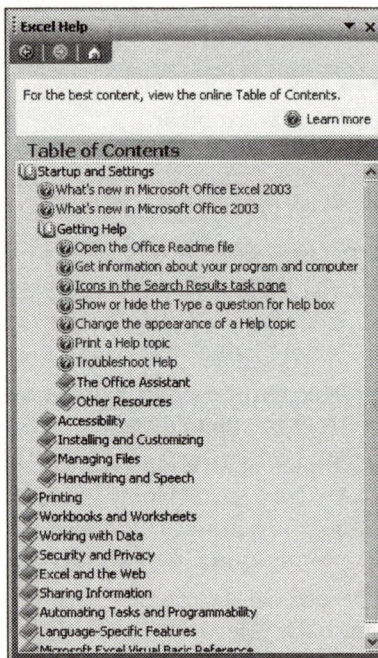

Excel Help ▼ ✕

For the best content, view the online Table of Contents.
🌐 Learn more

**Table of Contents**
📘 Startup and Settings
  📄 What's new in Microsoft Office Excel 2003
  📄 What's new in Microsoft Office 2003
  📘 Getting Help
    📄 Open the Office Readme file
    📄 Get information about your program and computer
    📄 Icons in the Search Results task pane
    📄 Show or hide the Type a question for help box
    📄 Change the appearance of a Help topic
    📄 Print a Help topic
    📄 Troubleshoot Help
    📄 The Office Assistant
    📄 Other Resources
  📄 Accessibility
  📄 Installing and Customizing
  📄 Managing Files
  📄 Handwriting and Speech
📄 Printing
📄 Workbooks and Worksheets
📄 Working with Data
📄 Security and Privacy
📄 Excel and the Web
📄 Sharing Information
📄 Automating Tasks and Programmability
📄 Language-Specific Features
📄 Microsoft Excel Visual Basic Reference

## Help pages

On a Help page some text may be blue. This indicates a 'hot spot' that can display some information.

The most common types of hot spots are:

* Bulleted item – displays a list of instructions.

* Embedded item – gives (usually in green) an explanation or definition of the word or phrase.

* Tip – suggested Help.

* Show All – expands or collapses all the hot spots on the page.

When you've finished exploring the Help system, click the **Close** button ☒ at the top right of the window.

**At the top of a Help Page:**

⊞  Tiles the Help Task Pane and the Help page.

▣  Un-tiles the Help Task Pane and the Help page.

⇦  Takes you back through the Help pages viewed.

⇨  Takes you forward through the Help pages viewed.

🖶  Prints the Help page.

# 1.9 Office Assistant

You can use the Assistant as a 'front end' to the Help system.

1 Open the **Help** menu and choose **Show Office Assistant**.

2 Click on the Office Assistant to display the dialog bubble.

> **What would you like to do?**
>
> how do I sort data
>
> Options      Search

3 Type in your question.

4 Click **Search**.

The Search Results Task Pane will open – click on a topic to display the Help page.

The Office Assistant can remain visible as you work on your document, or you can hide it and call on it as required. If you opt to leave it displayed, drag it to an area of your screen where it doesn't obscure your work.

- If you leave the Office Assistant displayed, left-click on it any time you want to ask a question.

- To hide the Office Assistant, right-click on it and choose **Hide** from the pop-up menu.

## To customize the Office Assistant

You can customize the Office Assistant to take on a different appearance, or behave in a different way.

1 Right-click on the Assistant and the **Options** button.

> **Office Assistant**
>
> Gallery | Options
>
> You can scroll through the different assistants by using the <Back and Next> buttons. When you are finished selecting your assistant, click the OK button.
>
> Time to play cat and mouse?
>
> Name: Links
> If you're on the prowl for answers in Office, Links can chase them down for you.
>
> <Back      Next>
>
> OK      Cancel

**To change its appearance:**

**2** Select the **Gallery** tab and browse through the options available (use the **Next** and **Back** buttons to move through the various 'guises').

**3** If you find an Assistant you would like to use, click **OK**.

• To leave the Assistant as it was, click **Cancel**.

**To change its behaviour:**

**4** Select the **Options** tab and set the options as required – click on an option to switch it on or off. A tick in a box means an option is selected, an empty box means it isn't.

• If you don't want to use the Office Assistant, you can switch it off on the **Options** tab – simply deselect the *Use the Office Assistant* checkbox.

**5** Click **OK** to set the options selected or **Cancel** to leave things as they were.

## Tips

If you select any 'Show Tips About' options on the Options tab in the Customize dialog box, the Office Assistant will constantly monitor your actions. If it thinks that it has a tip that may be useful to you, a light bulb will light up beside it. To read its tip, click the bulb.

## ScreenTips

If you point to any tool on a displayed toolbar, a ScreenTip will probably appear to describe the purpose of the tool. If no ScreenTips appear, you can easily switch them on.

1  Right-click on any toolbar.

2  Choose **Customize...** from the shortcut menu.

3  In the **Customize** dialog box select the **Options** tab.

4  To switch the ScreenTips on, select the *Show ScreenTips on* **toolbars** option (deselect this option to switch them off).

5  Click **Close.**

## Dialog box Help

When you access a dialog box, e.g. **Customize** shown here, you can get Help directly from within it.

To get Help on an item in a dialog box:

1  Click the **Help** button 🛈 at the right of the title bar.

2  Navigate through the Help system to find the Help you need.

# 1.10 Help on the Internet

If you can't find the Help you are looking for in the offline Help system, visit Microsoft Office Online to get updated Help files, answers to frequently asked questions on Excel, tips, technical support and articles on Excel and Office.

**1** Open the **Help** menu.

**2** Choose **Microsoft Office Online**.

**3** Navigate your way through the Help pages until you find the information required.

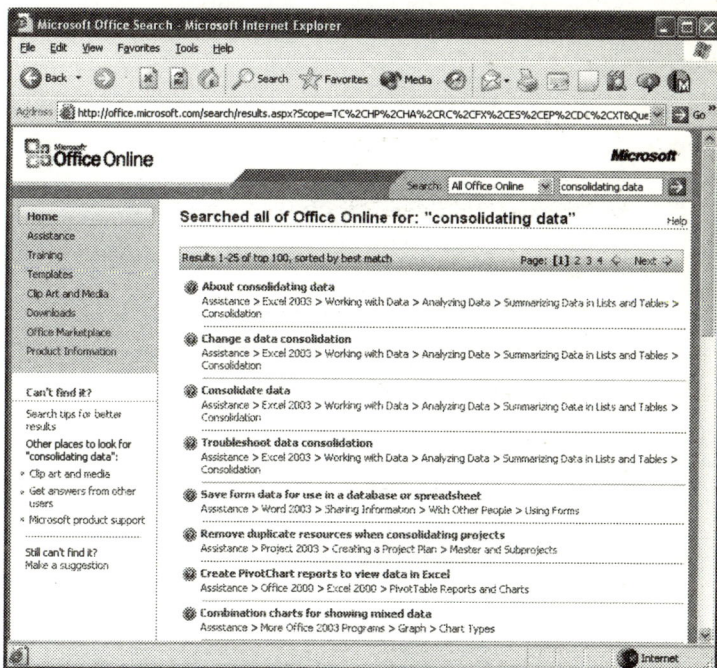

* You can access Microsoft Office Online from the **Search** options at the bottom of the Search Results Task Pane.

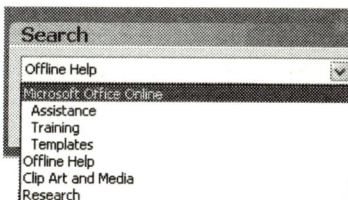

# 1.11 Exiting Excel

When you have finished working in Excel you must close the application down – don't just switch off your computer!

**To exit Excel:**

* Open the **File** menu and choose **Exit**.

Or

* Click the **Close** button ⊠ in the right-hand corner of the application title bar.

If you have been working on a workbook, but have not saved it, you will be prompted to do so – see '*Save a workbook*', in section 2.2.

---

## Summary

In this chapter we have discussed:

* The minimum software and hardware requirements

* The installation procedure for Excel

* Accessing the package through the Start menu

* The Excel screen

* The difference between workbooks and worksheets

* Utilizing the menu system using the mouse and the keyboard

* The offline and online Help system

* Exiting Excel

# 02 basic excel skills

**In this chapter you will learn:**

- some spreadsheet jargon
- about workbooks
- about entering and editing text, data and formulas
- about formatting cells
- how to move and copy data and formulas

## Aims of this chapter

This chapter introduces the basic skills you will need to work in Excel. By the time you have completed this chapter you will have created a simple worksheet and you will know how to create, edit, save, print, open and close a workbook.

# 2.1 Spreadsheet jargon

Before going any further, spend a little time getting familiar with some of the jargon you will encounter. There's nothing difficult about it – once you know what it means!

### Rows, columns and cells

The worksheet area consists of rows, columns and cells. Rows are identified by the numbers down the left side of the worksheet area. Row 7 is highlighted in the illustration below. There are *lots* of rows on a worksheet – 65,536 in fact!

Columns are identified by letters along the top of the worksheet area. Column E is highlighted in the illustration below. After Z, columns are labelled AA to AZ, then BA to BZ, and so on to IV, giving 256 columns in all.

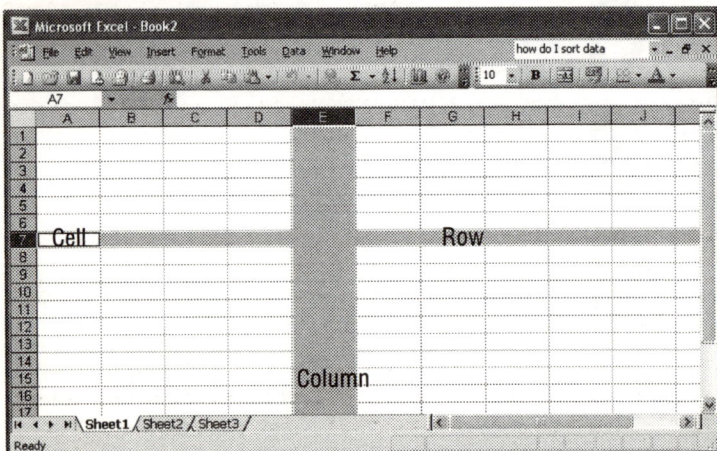

Where a row and column intersect you have a cell. Cells are identified using a cell *name* or *address*. A cell address consists of the column letter followed by the row number of the column and row that intersect to create the cell.

Cell A1, B9, C3, D6 and F3 have been highlighted in the screenshot below.

## Text, data, formulas and functions

The cells in your worksheet will eventually hold text, numeric data, formulas or functions.

*Text* is used for titles or narrative to describe the figures you are presenting – worksheet headings, column and row labels will usually be text entries.

*Numeric data* means the figures that appear in your worksheet. The data may be entered through the keyboard, or it may be generated as the result of a calculation.

*Formulas* are used to perform calculations on the numeric data in your worksheet (see section 2.10 and Chapter 5). Formulas are used to add the value in one cell to that in another or multiply the values in different cells, etc. Some of your formulas will be very basic while others may be quite complex.

*Functions* are predefined formulas that perform simple or complex calculations. There are many different kinds of functions in Excel – statistical, logical, financial, database, engineering – and many more (see Chapters 5 and 6). You're bound to find some useful ones, whatever type of data you work with.

# 2.2 File handling

In Excel, a file is called a workbook. Each new workbook you create is automatically given a temporary file name – *Book1*, *Book2*, etc. The name appears on the workbook Title bar.

When you open Excel a new workbook is created automatically. There are several ways in which you can create new workbooks and open existing ones in Excel.

### New workbook

To create a new blank workbook:

* Click the New tool ▢ on the Standard toolbar.

To create a workbook based on an existing workbook or template:

1 Open the File menu and choose New...

2 Select From existing workbook... or On my computer... from the New Workbook Task Pane.

### Open a workbook

To open a workbook without the Task Pane:

1 Click the Open tool ▣ on the Standard toolbar.

Or

* Open the File menu and choose Open.

2 In the Open dialog box, locate and select the workbook.

3 Click Open.

If the workbook you want to open has been used recently, you may find it in the list of recently-used files in the File menu.

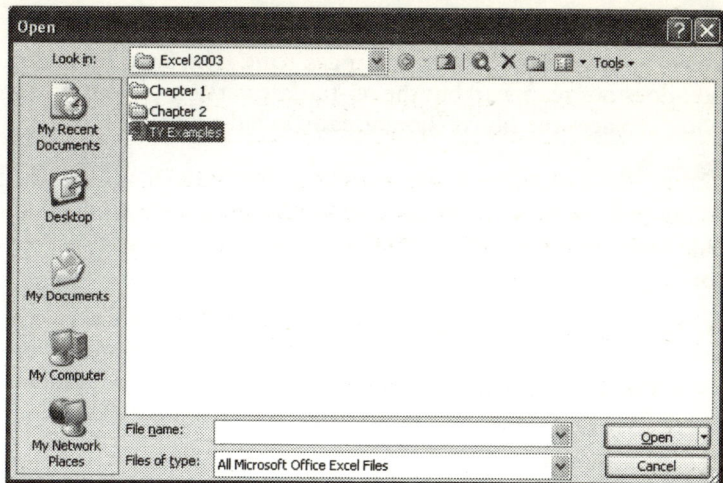

## Save a workbook

At some stage you must save your workbook to disk (if you don't you will lose it when you switch off your computer). When you save your workbook, you should give it a file name that reflects its contents rather than use the *Bookx* temporary name.

To save your workbook:

1  Click the *Save* tool 🔲 on the Standard toolbar.
2  At the *Save As* dialog box, locate the folder in which you wish to save your workbook (usually *My Documents*).
3  Enter the name in the File name: field.
4  Leave the *Save as type:* at *Microsoft Office Excel Workbook*.
5  Click *Save*.

You are returned to your workbook. The new name of the workbook appears on the workbook Title bar.

You can save your workbook at any time – you don't need to wait until you've entered all your data. I suggest you save your workbook regularly – and remember to resave it when you make changes to it. If you haven't saved your workbook, and your computer crashes or you have a power failure, you may lose any unsaved data.

Once a workbook has been saved, simply click the *Save* tool
when you want to save any changes to it. The Save As dialog
box does not reappear, but the up-to-date version of your workbook replaces the old version already saved to disk.

## Save As

There may be times that you save a workbook, edit it, then decide that you want to save the edited workbook but also keep
the original version of the workbook on disk.

If you don't want to overwrite the old version of a workbook
with the new edited version, save the new version using a different file name. You can save your workbook to the same folder if
you want to, or you can select a different drive and/or folder.

1 Open the *File* menu and choose *Save As*.

2 The *Save As* dialog box will appear again. Enter a new name
in the *File name:* field.

3 Click *Save*.

♦ If you save the new version of the file into the same folder as
the old one, you must use a different file name.

## Password protection

If you wish to password protect your workbook (so that no one
can open or edit the workbook unless they know the password)
you can do so from the *Save As* dialog box.

1 Click the **Tools** button on the *Save As* dialog box toolbar
and choose *General Options*.

2 Enter the password(s).

3 Click *OK*.

4 Re-enter the password(s) at the prompt.

5 Click *OK*.

**Closing your workbook**

* Open the File menu and choose Close.

Or

* Click the Close button ⊠ in the top right of the window.

# 2.3 Moving around your worksheet

Before you can enter anything into a cell, you must make the cell you want to work on *active*. To make a single cell active, you must select it. You can easily move onto any cell (thus making it active) using either the keyboard or the mouse.

The active cell has a dark border. The address of the active cell appears in the Name box to the left of the formula bar.

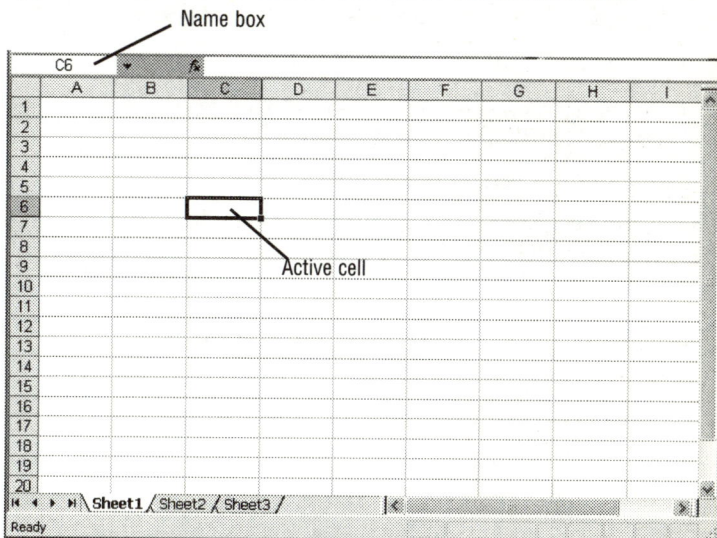

To move to a cell using the mouse:

* Click on the cell (you may need to use the horizontal or vertical scrollbars to bring the cell into view).

To move to a cell using the keyboard:

* To move right or left one column, or up or down one row at a time use the right, left, up and down arrow keys.

- To move to the last occupied cell in any direction, hold down [Ctrl] and press the arrow key that points that way.

- To move onto the cell directly below the one that is currently active press [Enter].

You can also go to a specific cell, if you know its address.

**To go to a specific cell:**

1 Press [F5].

2 Enter the address of the cell you want to go to in the **Reference** field of the **Go To** dialog box.

3 Click OK.

| Go To | ? X |
|---|---|
| Go to: | |
| | |
| Reference: | |
| IV65536 | |
| Special... | OK | Cancel |

**To return to cell A1 from anywhere in your worksheet:**

- Hold down [Ctrl] and press [Home].

**To move to the end of the work area on your worksheet** (the last cell you have worked on, rather than cell IV65536):

- Hold down [Ctrl] and press [End].

Check out *Keyboard shortcuts* in the online Help to see if there are any others that you would find useful.

## 2.4 Selecting ranges of cells

You will often work on more than one cell at a time in Excel. You may need to format a group of cells in a particular way or copy or move a group, or apply a function to a group.

A group of cells is called a cell range. Cell ranges are identified by the first cell address in the range, then a colon, followed by the last cell address, e.g. A1:A7, C3:D12, F5:H7. These ranges are highlighted in the picture opposite.

### Using the mouse

To *select a group of adjacent cells:*

1 Click and drag over the range of cells you wish to select.

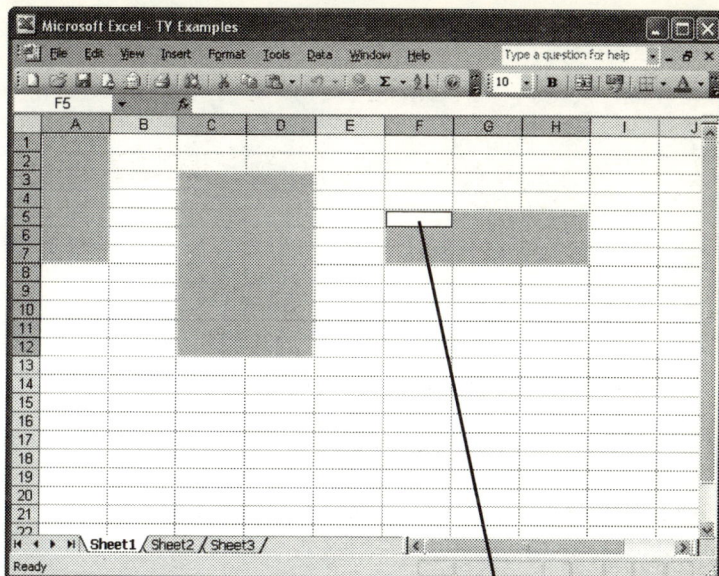

Note that the first cell selected is not highlighted

Or

**1** Click on a cell in one corner of the range you wish to select.

**2** Hold down [*Shift*].

**3** Click on the cell in the diagonally opposite corner of the range you want to select.

To *select a* **row or rows**:

+ Click the row number to the left of the row you want to select.

Or

+ Drag down over the row numbers to select several rows.

To *select a* **column or columns**:

+ Click the letter at the top of the column you want to select.

Or

+ Drag across the column letters to select several columns.

To *select the* **whole worksheet**:

+ Click the box at the top of the row numbers, and left of the column letters.

Select whole sheet          Select columns

Select rows

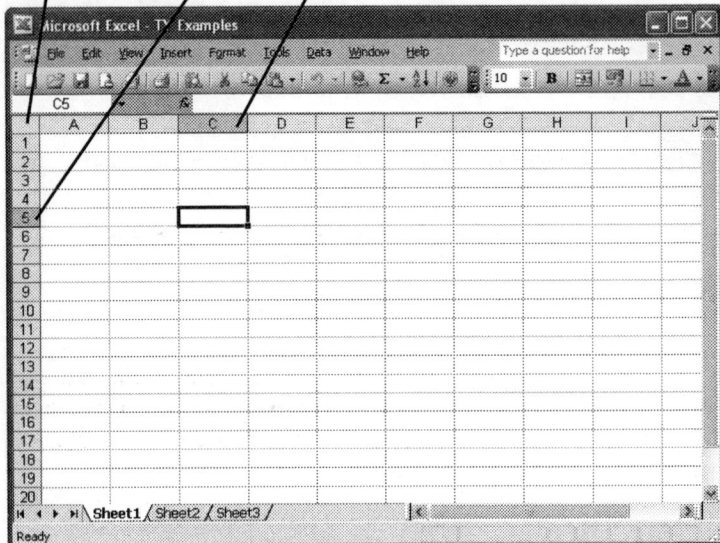

To select a range of non-adjacent cells:

1 Click on one of the cells you want to select.
2 Hold down [Ctrl].
3 Click on each of the other cells you want to select.

To deselect a range of cells:

+ Click on any cell outside the range.

## Using the keyboard

To select a group of adjacent cells:

1 Click in a cell that will be in the corner of the range you wish to select.
2 Hold down [Shift].
3 Press the arrow keys to move to the cell in the diagonally opposite corner, and release [Shift].

To deselect a range of cells:

+ Press one of the arrow keys.

# 2.5 Entering text and numeric data

Each time you start Excel a new workbook is created. To use this new workbook, close the Getting Started Task Pane and enter your data. Entering text or data into your worksheet is easy.

1 Select the cell you want to enter text or data into.

2 Type in the text or data – the text or data will appear in the formula bar as well as in the active cell.

3 Press [Enter] or click the 'tick' button to the left of the formula bar when you've completed the cell.

Things to note when entering numeric data:

+ If you have adjusted the width of a column (see section 2.7) then enter data that is too large for the width, the cell will display ######## signs instead of the figures. When this happens you must either change the number format (see section 2.9) or adjust the width again (see section 2.7).

+ Numbers align by default to the right (see section 3.2).

Things to note when entering text:

+ Text that doesn't fit into a single cell will 'spill over' into the cell to the right if that one is empty.

Formula bar

- Text that doesn't fit into a single cell will be only partially displayed if the cell to the right is not empty. You will need to widen the column (see section 2.7) to display all of the text.
- Text aligns by default to the left of a cell (see section 3.2).

## 2.6 Editing text and numeric data

If you make an error when entering data, you can fix things by:

- Deleting the contents of the cell.
- Replacing the contents of the cell.
- Editing the contents or the cell.

To *delete the contents of a cell* (or *cells*):

**1** Select the cell (or cells) whose contents you want to erase.

**2** Press [Delete] on your keyboard.

To *replace all the contents of a cell*:

**1** Select the cell whose contents you want to replace.

**2** Type in the text or data that should be in the cell.

To *edit the contents of a cell*:

**1** Select the cell whose contents you want to edit.

**2** Click in the Formula bar.

**3** Edit the cell contents as required (you can move right and left using the arrow keys, delete characters using [Delete] or [Backspace], or enter text or data through the keyboard).

**4** Press [Enter] on your keyboard when you've finished editing to return to the sheet.

Or

**1** Double-click in the cell whose contents you want to edit – this places the insertion point within the cell.

**2** Edit the cell contents as required.

**3** Press [Enter] when you've finished editing.

## Examples in this book

In this book we will use several different worksheets to illustrate various features in Excel. I suggest you enter these examples into a workbook and use them as practice material. You can then experiment with the features.

### Simon's Sports

The first worksheet will display a list of items that are in a sale in Simon's Sports. We will use this worksheet to demonstrate some of Excel's features as you work through the rest of this chapter. Enter the text displayed in the worksheet below and build up the worksheet as you work through the rest of the chapter.

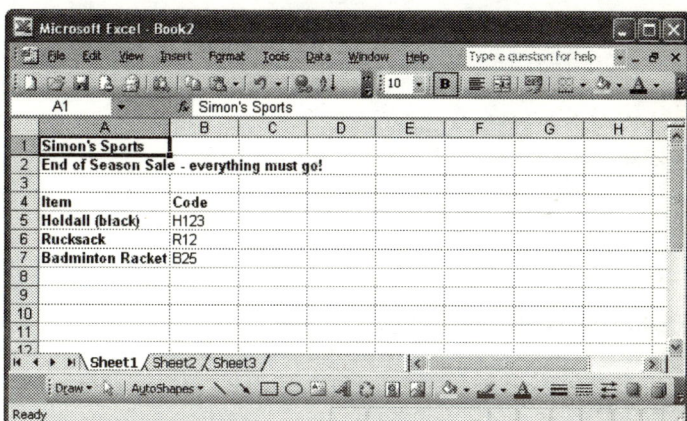

# 2.7 Column width

If the text you are entering into a cell is more than the column width will accommodate, you must do something about it if you want it to be fully visible.

Sometimes – particularly with main headings at the top of a worksheet – it doesn't matter if the text spills over into the cells to the right. However, when entering column headings or row labels each entry should occupy a single cell – with no overspill into the next column.

One way to make text fit into a single cell is to adjust the column width.

## Manual adjustment

To change the width of a column:

* In the column heading row, click and drag the vertical line to the right of the column whose width you want to change – in this example we need to widen column A.

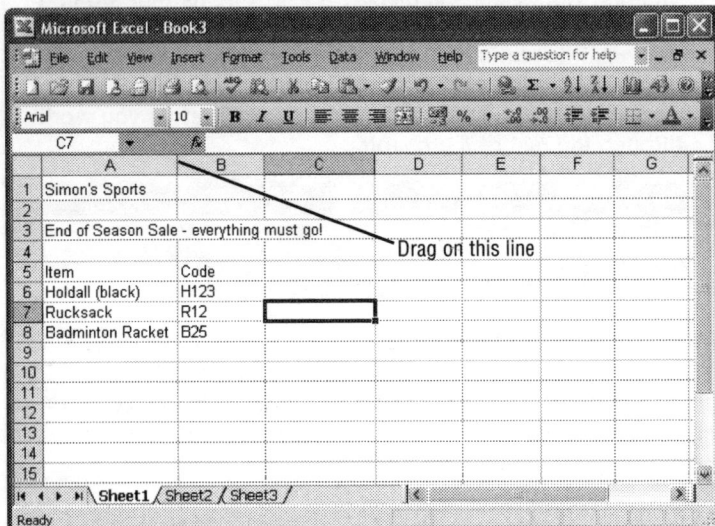

## AutoFit

You can get Excel to automatically adjust the width of the column to fit the entries within it.

To adjust the column width automatically:

* In the column heading row, double-click the vertical line to the right of the column you want to adjust.

## Format menu

You can also adjust the column width from the Format menu.

To set a specific column width:

1 Select any cell in the column you want to adjust.
2 Open the Format menu and choose Column.
3 Choose Width.

**4** Complete the **Column Width** dialog box – the value is the number of characters that will fit in the standard font.

**5** Click **OK**.

To *automatically adjust a column's width*:

**1** Select the cell that will determine the width for your column.

**2** Open the **Format** menu and choose **Column**.

**3** Click *AutoFit Selection*.

To *change the default column width for your columns*:

**1** Open the **Format** menu and choose **Column**.

**2** Choose *Standard Width*.

**3** Set the size in the *Standard Width* dialog box.

**4** Click **OK**.

## 2.8 Text wrap within a cell

Sometimes it is best to force a text entry to *wrap* within a cell, rather than have to widen a column to accommodate it. This applies particularly to headings. Consequently it may be useful to set the *Text wrap within cell* option for the row that contains your column headings.

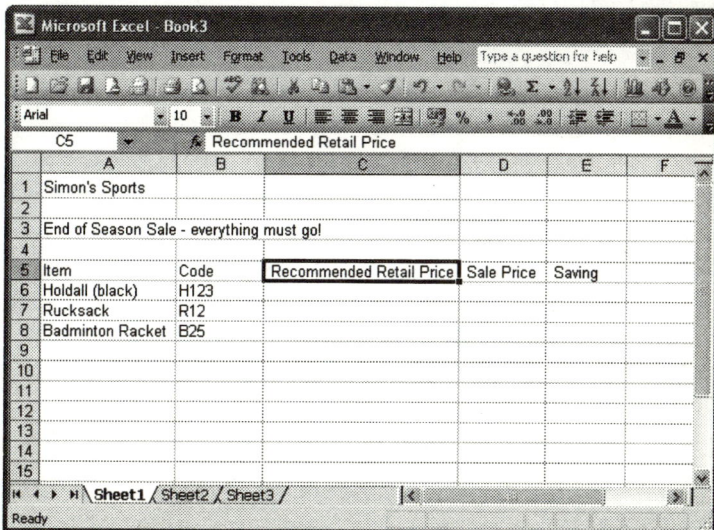

In the last example, monetary values will eventually go in the *Recommended Retail Price* column and will only take up 6 or 7 characters. To widen the column to accommodate the heading would result in a strange looking layout in our final worksheet.

To specify that text should wrap within a row of cells:

1 Select the row you want to set the text wrap option for.

2 Open the Format menu and choose Cells...

3 Select the Alignment tab.

4 Select the Wrap text checkbox.

5 Click OK.

Experiment with other options to see what effect they have

Column heading with **Wrap text** turned on

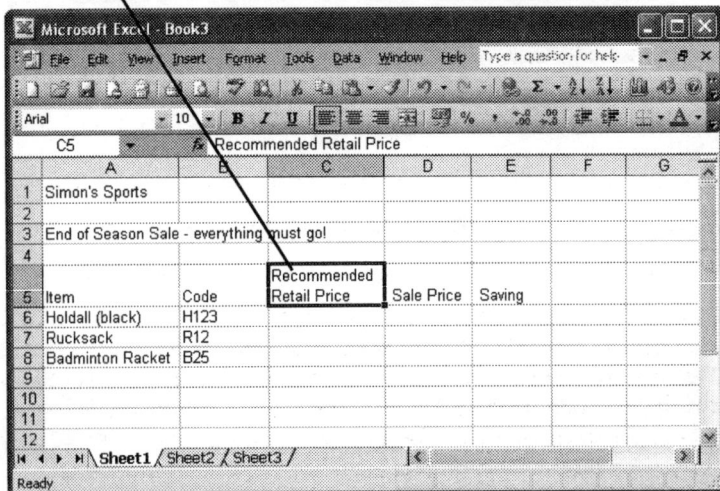

Adjust the column widths as necessary to get the effect you want.

- If the row height does not adjust automatically to accommodate the text when it wraps, choose Row from the Format menu, then select AutoFit.

### Shrink to fit

If the contents of a cell are just *too* wide for the column width, and you don't want to widen the column, you can get the contents of the cell to 'shrink to fit'.

1 Select the cell whose contents you want to shrink to fit.
2 Open the Format menu and choose Cells...
3 On the Alignment tab, select the Shrink to fit checkbox and click OK.

## 2.9 Number formats

A lot of the data entered into a worksheet is currency. Most of the times that you enter currency values, you will want the appropriate currency symbol to precede the figure.

To place a currency symbol in front of a figure:

- Format the cells to display the entry in a currency format.

Or

- Enter the symbol through the keyboard.

If you enter your figures through the numeric keypad, it's probably easiest to format the cells to display the figures as currency.

You can format cells *before* or *after* you enter your text or data.

To format the cells to display the figures in currency format:

1 Select the cells you want to format (see section 2.4 above).

2 Click the Currency tool ![currency tool] on the Formatting toolbar.

The Formatting toolbar has some other tools to help you format numbers – Percent Style, Comma Style, Increase and Decrease Decimal (these two change the number of decimal places displayed). Other number formats can be found on the Number tab of the Format Cells dialog box – have a look to see if any would be useful to you. The Euro is in the *Currency* category.

```
Microsoft Excel - Book3                                                 □□×
File  Edit  View  Insert  Format  Tools  Data  Window  Help   Type a question for help   _ ₿ ×
Arial          ▼ 10  ▼  B  I  U  ≡ ≡ ≡ ▦  ₩ %  , +.0 .00  ≡ ≡  ▦ ▼ A ▼
     E6       ▼        ƒx
          A           B          C           D         E         F         G
1  Simon's Sports
2
3  End of Season Sale - everything must go!
4
                            Recommended
5  Item            Code     Retail Price    Sale Price  Saving
6  Holdall (black)  H123    £      15.50  £     9.99
7  Rucksack        R12     £      16.99  £     9.99
8  Badminton Racket B25    £      24.00  £    15.99
9  Squash Racket   S44-A   £      27.75  £    19.99
10
11
12
13
14
H ◄ ► H \ Sheet1 / Sheet2 / Sheet3 /           │◄
Ready
```

**To apply a format from the Format Cells dialog box:**

**1** Select the cells you want to format.

**2** Open the **Format** menu and choose *Cells...*

**3** Select the **Number** tab.

**4** Choose a category from the list.

**5** Complete the dialog box as required – exactly what appears in it depends on the category you select.

**6** Click OK.

♦ **To enter the € symbol** through the keyboard, hold down [*Alt*] and type 0128 on the Number Pad. (Check out the online Help for more information on Euros.)

## 2.10 Formulas

Any cell in your workbook, which will contain a figure that has been calculated using other entries in your workbook, should have a formula or function in it (do *not* do your calculations on a calculator, then type the answer in to your workbook).

Formulas allow you to add, subtract, multiply, divide and work out percentages of the values in cells.

*Operators used in formulas are:*

| | | | |
|---|---|---|---|
| + | Add | – | Subtract |
| / | Divide | * | Multiply |
| % | Percentage | | |

In our example we are going to use a formula to work out how much a customer will save if they buy something in the sale.

To work out the saving for the first item in the list (the holdall), we need to subtract the sale price (the figure in cell D6) from the recommended retail price (in cell C6). The result of this calculation should be displayed in cell E6, in the *Saving* column.

To *enter the formula:*

1 Select the cell that will contain the result of the calculation (E6 in this example).

2 Type '=' (to tell Excel we're entering a formula).

3 Click on cell C6 (the recommended retail price cell for the item).

♦ The cell address appears in the Formula bar *and* in the current cell.

4 Type '–' (we're subtracting).

5 Click on cell D6 (the cell containing the *sale price* figure).

6 Press [Enter].

♦ The result of the calculation will appear in cell E6.

At step 3 and step 5 above, I suggested you click on the cell you want to use in your formula. If you prefer, you can enter the cell address manually by typing the coordinates into your formula instead.

## Simple formula examples

| | |
|---|---|
| =A7/B6 | Divide the figure in A7 by the figure in B6 |
| =D22*12 | Multiply the figure in D22 by 12 |
| =C7*25% | Calculate 25% of the figure in C7 |

## Order of precedence

If there is a mixture of operators in a formula, Excel will deal with the multiplication and division *before* it deals with the addition and subtraction.

=A4+C7*D7

Multiply the figure in C7 by the one in D7, and add the answer to the figure in A4

=A1+B2/C3+D4*E5-F2

Add to the figure in A1, the result of dividing the figure in B2 by that in C3, then add the result of multiplying the figure in D4 by that in E5, then subtract the figure in F2 (phew!).

## Parentheses

Some formulas can become quite long and complicated – and tricky to follow! If you want to force the order in which a formula is worked out, or even just make a long formula easier to read, you must use parentheses ( ).

In the example below, the operation in each set of parentheses is solved *before* working through the formula.

=(A1+B2)/C3+(D4*(E5-F2))

| | |
|---|---|
| Add A1 to B2 | we'll call this X |
| Subtract F2 from E5 | we'll call this Y |
| Multiply Y by D4 | we'll call this Z |

To get the final result:

Divide X by C3 then add Z

I hope you followed that!

To help you remember, think BODMAS! Brackets Of (powers) Division and Multiplication, then Addition and Subtraction. Work from left to right and *never* move the entries you are calculating.

## 2.11 AutoFill

In Simon's Sports sale worksheet, we could work down the column entering the formula for each *Saving* cell. However, a much quicker way to achieve the same result is to use AutoFill. AutoFill allows you to *copy* a formula from one cell into adjacent cells – to the right, left, up or down.

To AutoFill *the formula in* E6 *to the other Saving cells:*

**1** Select E6.

**2** Position the pointer over the bottom right corner of the cell – the Fill handle (a small black cross) should appear.

**3** Drag the black cross down over the other *Saving* cells.

When you release the mouse, the formula in cell E6 will be copied to the cells you dragged over.

If you click on each cell in the saving column and keep an eye on the Formula bar, you will notice that Excel has automatically changed the cell addresses in the formula *relative* to the position you have copied the formula to. Neat trick!

| | A | B | C | D | E | F | G |
|---|---|---|---|---|---|---|---|
| | Microsoft Excel - Book3 | | | | | | |
| | File Edit View Insert Format Tools Data Window Help | | | | Type a question for help | | |
| | Arial | 10 | B I U | | | | |
| | E6 | | = =C6-D6 | | | | |
| 1 | Simon's Sports | | | | | | |
| 2 | | | | | | | |
| 3 | End of Season Sale - everything must go! | | | | | | |
| 4 | | | | | | | |
| 5 | Item | Code | Recommended Retail Price | Sale Price | Saving | | |
| 6 | Holdall (black) | H123 | £      15.50 | £      9.99 | £     5.51 | | |
| 7 | Rucksack | R12 | £      16.99 | £      9.99 | | | |
| 8 | Badminton Racket | B25 | £      24.00 | £    15.99 | | | |
| 9 | Squash Racket | S44-A | £      27.75 | £    19.99 | | | |
| 10 | | | | | | | |
| 11 | | | | | | | |
| 12 | | | | | | | |

Sheet1 / Sheet2 / Sheet3 /

Drag outside selection to extend series or fill; drag inside to clear                NUM

When you AutoFill text or data, a smart tag appears below the data that you have copied. Click the smart tag to see the Auto-Fill options. If you don't want the default, click the option required.

| Copy Cells |
| Fill Formatting Only |
| Fill Without Formatting |

AutoFill can be a real time-saver in some situations. Try these.

To enter labels for each month or day of the week:

1 Enter the first month or day you want to use into the appropriate cell – 'January' or 'Jan', 'Wednesday' or 'Wed'.

2 AutoFill the contents of that cell across the columns or down the rows – Excel will automatically complete the other cells.

To enter a number sequence, e.g. 1, 2, 3, 4 or 0, 50, 100, etc.:

1 Enter the first two numbers in two adjacent cells.

2 Select both cells.

3 AutoFill down the rows or across the columns.

If you want to enter dates, you can use the Fill option. The date can be incremented using every day of the week (day), weekdays only (Monday to Friday), months or years.

1 Enter the first date in your series.

2 Click and drag the Fill Handle using the *right* mouse button.

Screenshot of Microsoft Excel - Book3:

|  | A | B | C | D | E | F | G | H |
|---|---|---|---|---|---|---|---|---|
| 1 |  |  |  | Fill Weekdays | Step Value 10 | Fill Years | Fill Months |  |
| 2 | Jan | January | Monday | MON | 10 | 01/01/2003 | 01/01/2004 |  |
| 3 | Feb | February | Tuesday | TUE | 20 | 01/01/2004 | 01/02/2004 |  |
| 4 | Mar | March | Wednesday | WED | 30 | 01/01/2005 | 01/03/2004 |  |
| 5 | Apr | April | Thursday | THU | 40 | 01/01/2006 | 01/04/2004 |  |
| 6 | May | May | Friday | FRI | 50 | 01/01/2007 | 01/05/2004 |  |
| 7 | Jun | June | Saturday | MON | 60 | 01/01/2008 | 01/06/2004 |  |
| 8 | Jul | July | Sunday | TUE | 70 | 01/01/2009 | 01/07/2004 |  |
| 9 | Aug | August | Monday | WED | 80 | 01/01/2010 | 01/08/2004 |  |
| 10 | Sep | September | Tuesday | THU | 90 | 01/01/2011 | 01/09/2004 |  |
| 11 | Oct | October | Wednesday | FRI | 100 | 01/01/2012 | 01/10/2004 |  |
| 12 | Nov | November | Thursday | MON | 110 | 01/01/2013 | 01/11/2004 |  |
| 13 | Dec | December | Friday | TUE | 120 | 01/01/2014 | 01/12/2004 |  |
| 14 |  |  |  |  |  |  |  |  |
| 15 |  |  |  |  |  |  |  |  |

**3** When you release the button, a pop-up menu appears.

**4** Select the fill option you require – **Fill Days, Fill Weekdays, Fill Months** or **Fill Years**.

Examples of some of the Fill options are displayed on page 38.

- Column A and B show different month formats AutoFilled.
- Column C and D show different day formats AutoFilled.
- Column E shows figures with an increment of 10 AutoFilled.
- Column F has been completed using the Fill Years option on the pop-up menu.
- Column G has been completed using the Fill Months option on the pop-up menu.

## 2.12 Another worksheet!

Use this example to get some more practice. Enter the text and data below into a different worksheet in your workbook. To select a different worksheet, click the sheet tab – Sheet1, Sheet2, Sheet 3, etc. to the left of the horizontal scroll bar. It doesn't matter which sheet you use. This example is for a stock value table for *Screw the Nut plc*. Use the following notes to help you get the layout and formulas correct.

The Microsoft Excel window shows cell G11 selected with formula =G6+G7+G8+G9:

| | A | B | C | D | E | F | G | H |
|---|---|---|---|---|---|---|---|---|
| 1 | SCREW THE NUT PLC | | | | | | | |
| 2 | | | | | | | | |
| 3 | Stock Value Table | | | | | | | |
| 4 | | | | | | | | |
| 5 | Part No | Description | Cost (trade) | Cost (retail) | Profit | Number in Stock | Value of Stock | |
| 6 | S1113 | Screwdriver set | £ 10.00 | £ 18.99 | £ 8.99 | 4 | £ 40.00 | |
| 7 | S2451 | Spanner set | £ 14.00 | £ 20.99 | £ 6.99 | 6 | £ 84.00 | |
| 8 | W2201 | Wrench & Grip set | £ 9.00 | £ 15.99 | £ 6.99 | 6 | £ 54.00 | |
| 9 | W3120 | Workman (B&D) | £ 60.00 | £ 75.00 | £ 15.00 | 3 | £ 180.00 | |
| 10 | | | | | | | | |
| 11 | | | | | | Total value of stock | £ 358.00 | |
| 12 | | | | | | | | |
| 13 | | | | | | | | |

Sheet1 / Sheet2 \ **Sheet4** / Sheet3 /

1 Enter the main headings and column headings, *Part No*, *De-scription*, *Cost (trade)*, *Cost (retail)*, *Profit* and *Number in Stock*.

2 Format row 5 to allow text wrap within the cells (see 2.8).

3 Format the data cells in the *Cost (trade)*, *Cost (retail)*, *Profit* and *Value of Stock* columns to display the figures as currency (see section 2.9).

4 Enter a formula to calculate the *Profit* figure. For the first item (screwdriver set) it would be **=D6-C6** (see section 2.10 for information on entering formulas).

5 The *Number in Stock* figures are centred in this example (see section 3.2).

6 Enter a formula to calculate the *Value of Stock* column. For the first item it would be **=C6*F6** (if you base the stock value on the trade price).

7 AutoFill the formulas down the columns (see section 2.11).

8 The *Total Value of Stock* figure could be calculated by entering the formula **=G6+G7+G8+G9** (you could also use the AutoSum function for this – see section 5.1).

## 2.13 Move or copy cell contents

If you enter text or data into your worksheet, and it's right but in the wrong place you can move it to where it should be (rather than delete it and retype it in the correct location).

**To move the contents of cells:**

1 Select the cells you want to move.

2 Click the **Cut** tool 📄 on the Standard toolbar.

3 Select the top leftmost cell of the range you want to move the text or data to.

4 Click the **Paste** tool 📄 on the Standard toolbar.

Or

1 Select the cells you want to move.

2 Point to the edge of the selected area – the mouse pointer displays four directional arrows.

3 Drag and drop the selected cells into the correct position.

**To copy the contents of cells:**

**1** Select the cells you want to copy.

**2** Click the **Copy tool**  on the Standard toolbar.

♦ A dotted line appears around the cells to be copied.

**3** Select the top leftmost cell of the range you want to copy the text or data to.

**4** Click the **Paste** tool on the Standard toolbar.

♦ For more than one copy, repeat steps 3 and 4 as required.

♦ Click the **Paste** smart tag to display the paste options.

**5** Press **[Esc]** to cancel the dotted line around the copied cells.

Or

**1** Select the cells you want to copy.

**2** Point to the edge of the selected area – the mouse pointer displays four directional arrows.

**3** Hold down **[Ctrl]** (the mouse pointer changes to a white arrow shape with + beside it) while you drag and drop the selected cells. (You must release the mouse button *before* **[Ctrl]** – if you don't, you'll end up moving the cells instead of copying them).

## Paste Special

When you copy and paste in Excel, you can be selective about what you paste – the functions, formatting, etc. Or you can paste data and add, subtract, multiply or divide it into existing data. Use Paste Special to do this.

**1** Copy or cut the data.

**2** Select the cell(s) that you want to paste the data into.

**3** Open the **Edit** menu.

**4** Choose **Paste Special**.

**5** Select the items you wish to paste e.g. **Values**.

**6** Choose the **Operation** to be performed (if any).

**7** Click **OK**.

## 2.14 Insert and delete rows and columns

As you build up your worksheet, you may discover that you have added a row or column that you don't require, or perhaps missed out a row or column that you do need.

**To insert a row:**

1  Select the row (see section 2.4) that will go *below* the row you are inserting.
2  Right-click within the selected area and choose **Insert** from the pop-up menu.

**To insert a column:**

1  Select the column (see section 2.4) that will go to the right of the column you are inserting.
2  Right-click within the selected area and choose **Insert**.

**To delete a row or column:**

1  Select the row or column you wish to delete.
2  Right-click within the selected area and choose **Delete**.

**To add or delete several rows or columns at the same time:**

1  Click and drag in the row or column label area to indicate how many rows or columns you want to insert or delete.
2  Right-click in the selected area and choose **Insert** or **Delete**.

## 2.15 Print preview and print

At some stage you will want to print your file. Before printing, it's a good idea to *preview* it. It takes practice to get a good fit, and you may find it useful to plan things in rough before you begin to draw up your worksheet. Page layout options are discussed in section 3.9.

### Print Preview

To preview your worksheet:

♦  Click the **Print Preview** tool on the Standard toolbar.

A preview of the current worksheet will be displayed in full-page view. It doesn't matter if you can't read what is on the screen – the preview is there to let you see how your worksheet will fit onto your paper. You get an idea of how well the data, white space, graphics, etc. will look on the page.

Simon's Sports

End of Season Sale - everything must go!

| Item | Code | Rec Retail Price | Sale Price | Saving |
|------|------|------|------|------|
| Holdall (black) | H123 | £15.50 | £9.99 | £5.51 |
| Rucksack | R12 | £16.99 | £9.99 | £7.00 |
| Badminton Racket | B25 | £24.00 | £15.99 | £8.01 |
| Squash Racket | S44-A | £27.75 | £19.99 | £7.76 |

Print Preview has its own toolbar

| Next | Previous | Zoom | Print... | Setup... | Margins | Page Break Preview | Close | Help |

### To change something when you see the preview:

**1** Click the **Close** tool on the **Print Preview** toolbar to return to your worksheet.

**2** Edit the worksheet as required.

**3** Preview again to see how it looks.

## Print

When you are happy with the preview, you can send it to print.

### To print from Print Preview:

**1** Click **Print...** on the Print Preview toolbar.

**2** Complete the **Print** dialog box – set **Number of copies** and **Print range** as required.

**3** Click **OK**.

### To print from worksheet (not in Print Preview):

♦ Click the **Print** tool on the Standard toolbar.

Your Print dialog box may be different – it depends upon the printer

One copy of the current worksheet will be sent to your printer.

## Print part of your worksheet

If you don't want to print all of your worksheet, you can print the area required on its own.

**To print part of your worksheet:**

**1** Select the range of cells you want to print.

**2** Open the **File** menu and choose **Print…**

**3** Select **Selection** from the **Print what** options.

**4** Click **OK**.

# Summary

In this chapter we have discussed:

- Spreadsheet jargon
- Cell names
- File handling – Save, Close, Open and New
- Moving around a worksheet
- Selection techniques – for rows, columns, adjacent and non-adjacent cells
- Entering text and numeric data
- Deleting, replacing and editing the contents of a cell
- Adjusting column widths
- Wrapping text within a cell and 'shrink to fit'
- Number formats
- Entering simple formulas
- Order of precedence and the use of parentheses
- AutoFill
- Moving and copying cells
- Inserting and deleting rows and columns
- Print Preview and Print

# 03
## formatting and layout

**In this chapter you will learn:**

- some more formatting options
- how to freeze panes
- how to split the screen
- how to set page layout options

## Aims of this chapter

In this chapter we will consider some of the cell formatting options that you can use to improve the presentation of a worksheet. We will also discuss ways of viewing different areas of a worksheet on the screen at the same time. Finally, to help you get your printouts exactly as you want them, we'll look at some of the page layout options.

# 3.1 Bold, italic and underline

You can make the contents of a cell (or cells) bold, italic or underlined using either the Formatting toolbar or keyboard shortcuts.

## Formatting toolbar

1 Select the cells you wish to make bold, italic or underline.

2 Click the **Bold** B , the *Italic* I and/or the Underline U tool on the Formatting toolbar.

3 Deselect the cells.

The bold, italics and underline tools are toggles – they are used to switch the formatting on or off.

**To remove bold, italics or underline formatting from a cell or cells:**

1 Select the cell(s) you wish to remove the formatting from.

2 Click the Bold, Italic and/or Underline tool.

3 Deselect the cells.

## Keyboard shortcuts

1 Select the cell or cells you wish to format.

2 Apply or remove the formatting with the keyboard shortcuts:

- **[Ctrl]-[B]** for bold
- **[Ctrl]-[I]** for italics
- **[Ctrl]-[U]** for underline

3 Deselect the cells.

# 3.2 Alignment

When entering text and data into your worksheet, the default alignment of text is to the left, and of numeric data is to the right. You can change the alignment of text or data within a cell if you wish, either before or after you enter it.

## Left, right and center

1 Select the cells required.

2 Click the **Align Left** tool ▤ on the Formatting toolbar to align the cell contents to the left.

Or

♦ Click the **Center** tool ▤ to align to the center.

Or

♦ Click the **Align Right** tool ▤ to align to the right.

## Center across selection

If you want to merge cells and centre the data in a cell across them, you can use the Merge and Center tool. This is useful when you want to centre a heading across several columns in your worksheet – perhaps the text in the title row.

**To centre text or data across several columns:**

**1** Select the range of cells you want to centre the text or data across, e.g. A3:E3.

**2** Click the **Merge and Center** tool ▣.

# 3.3 More formatting options

The default font used in Excel worksheets is Arial, the default font size is 10. You can change the font used or the font size if you wish.

The colours of the font and background can be set as required, and you can add borders to any or all sides of a block of cells if you want to make them really stand out.

**To change the font:**

**1** Select the cells.

**2** Click the drop-down arrow to the right of the **Font** field on the Formatting toolbar.

**3** Choose an alternative font from the list (use the scroll bar if necessary to bring the font required into view).

**To change the font size:**

**1** Select the cells you want to modify.

**2** Click the drop-down arrow to the right of the **Font Size** field on the Formatting toolbar.

**3** Choose an alternative font size from the list (use the scroll bar as necessary).

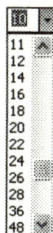

**To change the font colour:**

**1** Select the cell (or cells).

**2** Click the drop-down arrow to the right of the **Font Color** tool on the Formatting toolbar.

**3** Click on the colour you want to use.

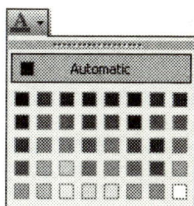

To change the background colour of a cell:

**1** Select the cell (or cells).

**2** Click the drop-down arrow to the right of the **Fill Color** tool.

**3** Click on the colour you want to use.

To **apply a border to a cell (or cells):**

**1** Select the cell (or cells).

**2** Click the drop-down arrow by the **Border** tool.

**3** Select the border effect you wish to use.

**4** Deselect your cell (or cells).

## Draw Border

If you choose **Draw Border** from the **Borders** options, the **Borders** toolbar appears and the mouse pointer becomes a pencil.

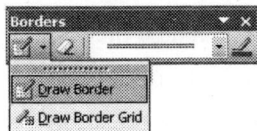

You can use this pencil to *draw* the borders in that you require.

To **create your border or border grid:**

**1** Choose **Draw Border** or **Draw Border Grid**.

**2** Select the **Line Style** and **Line Color** required using the tools on the toolbar.

**3** Click on the grid line where you want your border to appear (or drag along it if you want the border to cross a number of rows or columns).

• You can also create diagonal lines within a cell by dragging from one corner to the one diagonally opposite.

To **erase a border:**

**1** Click the **Erase Border** tool 📋.

**2** Click (or drag along) the border you want to remove.

## Format Cells dialog box

The formatting options can also be found in the Format Cells dialog box, on the Alignment, Font, Border and Patterns tabs.

**To display the dialog box:**

• Choose **Cells...** from the **Format** menu.

Experiment with the formatting options in your worksheets.

Angled text is useful for headings in narrow columns

There are more Font effects – and a preview – on the Font tab

All the border options are available on the Border tab

**Format Cells**

Number | Alignment | Font | Border | Patterns | Protection

Cell shading
Color:

No Color

Sample

Pattern: ▨ ▾

OK   Cancel

For customized fill
patterns, set the
shading, and the
pattern colour and style
on the Patterns tab

## 3.4 Format Painter

If you have applied several formatting options to a cell, and you
want to apply the same formatting to some other cells in your
worksheet you could save some time by using the Format Painter.
This allows you to copy the formatting from one cell, and paint
it on to other cells.

**To copy a format to a single cell, or to adjacent cells:**

**1** Select the cell that is formatted the way you want.

**2** Click the **Format Painter** tool 🖌 on the Standard toolbar.

**3** Click on the cell you want to apply the formatting to.

Or

♦ Click and drag over the cells that you want to apply the formatting to.

**To copy a format to non-adjacent cells:**

**1** Select the cell that is formatted the way you want.

**2** Double-click the **Format Painter** tool 🖌 on the Standard
toolbar – this 'locks' the Format Painter tool on.

**3** Click on each cell you want to apply the formatting to.

Or

- Drag over the cells you want to paint with the formatting.
4 Click the Format Painter tool again (or press [**Esc**]) to switch the Format Painter off when you've finished.

## 3.5 Conditional formatting

Conditional formatting is used to format a cell (or range of cells), if specific conditions are met.

You may have a list of figures, and decide that you want all those that are >=50000 displayed in red and italics, and all those figures that are <50000 displayed in green.

1 Select the cells that you want to apply the formatting to.

2 Open the **Format** menu and choose **Conditional Formatting...**

3 Set the **Condition 1** criterion.

4 Click the **Format...** button and set the formatting required.

5 Click **Add>>** so that you can specify another criteria (if required – you can specify up to 3 conditions).

6 Complete the dialog box as required.

7 Click **OK**.

## 3.6 Change the default font

If you don't want to use the default font of Arial, size 10, you can change it. *Once you have changed the default font, you must restart Excel before it will take effect.* Every new workbook you create will use the font you have specified as the default (until you change it again).

**To change the default font:**

1 Open the **Tools** menu and choose **Options**.

2 Select the **General** tab.

3 Set the **Standard font:** and **Size:** fields as required.

4 Click **OK**.

5 Click **OK** at the prompt that appears.

6 Exit Excel and restart it again for the change to take effect.

## 3.7 Freeze panes

Many of the worksheets you create will be considerably larger than will fit on to your computer screen. You will need to scroll vertically and horizontally to display the data you want to work with.

When you scroll your worksheet, the column headings or row labels will disappear off your screen as the other data appears.

This is often inconvenient, as you need to see the headings and labels to make sense of your data. In these situations you should *freeze* the heading columns and rows so that they stay in place and only the data cells scroll.

**To freeze a row (or rows):**

**1** Select the row below the ones you want to freeze.

**To freeze a column (or columns):**

♦ Select the column to the right of the ones to freeze.

**To freeze both a row (or rows) and column (or columns):**

♦ Select the cell below and to the right of where you want to freeze the panes.

**2** Open the **Window** menu.

**3** Choose **Freeze Panes**.

The worksheet will be divided into separate panes.

When you scroll through your worksheet horizontally, the column or columns you have frozen remain in view. When you scroll through your worksheet vertically the row or rows you have frozen will remain in view when the other data scrolls.

The heavy line indicates the edge of the frozen pane
Rows 1–4 are frozen

To **unfreeze panes:**

**1** Open the **Window** menu.

**2** Choose **Unfreeze Panes.**

## 3.8 Split screen

You may sometimes want to compare the data on one part of your worksheet with that on another – but the data ranges that you want to compare are in separate areas. When this happens, you should *split* your screen so that you can scroll each part independently, to bring the data you require into view.

### Split box

If you look at the top of the vertical scroll bar (above the up arrow), or to the right of the horizontal scroll bar (by the right arrow), you will see the *split boxes*. Use these to split your screen.

To **split your screen horizontally:**

◆ Drag the split box at the top of the vertical scroll bar down to where you want your split to be.

Horizontal split box

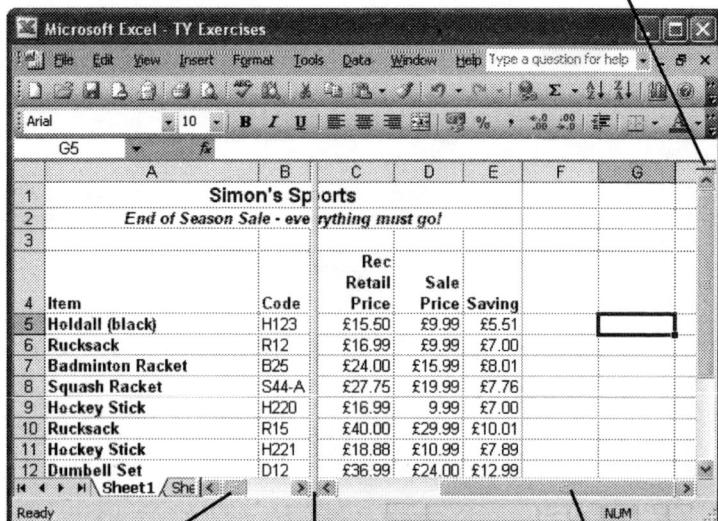

| | A | B | C | D | E | F | G |
|---|---|---|---|---|---|---|---|
| 1 | | Simon's Sports | | | | | |
| 2 | | End of Season Sale - everything must go! | | | | | |
| 3 | | | | | | | |
| 4 | Item | Code | Rec Retail Price | Sale Price | Saving | | |
| 5 | Holdall (black) | H123 | £15.50 | £9.99 | £5.51 | | |
| 6 | Rucksack | R12 | £16.99 | £9.99 | £7.00 | | |
| 7 | Badminton Racket | B25 | £24.00 | £15.99 | £8.01 | | |
| 8 | Squash Racket | S44-A | £27.75 | £19.99 | £7.76 | | |
| 9 | Hockey Stick | H220 | £16.99 | 9.99 | £7.00 | | |
| 10 | Rucksack | R15 | £40.00 | £29.99 | £10.01 | | |
| 11 | Hockey Stick | H221 | £18.88 | £10.99 | £7.89 | | |
| 12 | Dumbell Set | D12 | £36.99 | £24.00 | £12.99 | | |

Left pane scroll bar

Vertical split box, dragged across to split the screen

Right pane scroll bar

**To split your screen vertically:**

♦ Drag the split box at the right of the horizontal scroll bar along to where you want your split to be.

When your screen is split, you can scroll each pane independently to view the data you want to see.

**To remove a split:**

♦ Double-click the split.

# 3.9 Page layout

In Chapter 2 we discussed printing. We will now consider some ways in which you can change the appearance (or layout) of the printed sheet.

## Orientation

Pages are usually printed portrait (rather than landscape) on A4 paper.

**To change the orientation:**

**1** In a worksheet, open the **File** menu and choose **Page Setup**.

Or

♦ In Print Preview, click the **Setup...** button on the Print Preview toolbar to open the **Page Setup** dialog box.

**2** Select the **Page** tab.

**3** Choose the orientation option – *portrait* or *landscape*.

**4** Click **OK**.

## Scaling

If a worksheet is more than a page in size, you can specify the number of pages you want it to be printed on using the **Scaling** option.

**1** Open the **Page Setup** dialog box and select the **Page** tab.

**2** In the **Scaling** options, specify the number of pages wide and tall you want your worksheet to fit on.

**3** Click **OK**.

• Scaling is very useful if the last page of your worksheet contains only a small amount of data. You can specify that the worksheet prints on one page less than it really needs – Excel will scale it down to fit onto that number of pages.

## Page size

The default paper size is A4. You can select an alternative size.

1 Open the **Page Setup** dialog box and select the **Page** tab.
2 Choose the size required from the **Paper size** list.
3 Click **OK**.

## Margins

You can change the margin settings for a worksheet in either Page Setup or in Print Preview.

**To change the margins in the Page Setup dialog box:**

1 Open the **Page Setup** dialog box and select the **Margins** tab.
2 Specify the margins you want to use.
3 Click **OK**.

**To change the margins while in Print Preview:**

1 Click the **Margins** button on the Print Preview toolbar.
• The margins appear as dotted lines around your page.
2 Drag the margins to the position required.

## Page breaks

If a worksheet runs to more than one page, Excel will divide it by inserting automatic page breaks. Exactly where the breaks appear depends on the paper size, margin settings and scaling options. You can set your own horizontal and vertical breaks.

**To insert a horizontal page break:**

1 Select the row *below* where you want the page break to be.
2 Open the **Insert** menu and click **Page Break**.

**To insert a vertical page break:**

1 Select the column to the *right* of where you want the break.
2 Open the **Insert** menu and click **Page Break**.

**To insert a horizontal and vertical page break at the same time:**

**1** Select the cell immediately below and to the right of where you want to start a new page.

**2** Open the **Insert** menu and click **Page Break**.

**To move a page break:**

**1** Open the **View** menu and click **Page Break Preview**.

♦ The first time you do this a prompt appears – if you don't want it to appear again, select the checkbox and click **OK**.

**2** Drag the page break to its new position.

**To remove a page break:**

**1** Open the **View** menu and click **Page Break Preview**.

**2** Right-click on a cell below a horizontal page break or to the right of the vertical page break.

**3** Click **Remove Page Break** on the shortcut menu.

**4** Open the **View** menu and click **Normal** to return to your worksheet.

## Print column and row titles

If you are printing a worksheet with a list of data that runs over several pages, you might find the printout easier to interpret if you have the column and/or row titles repeated on each page.

**1** Open the **File** menu and choose **Page Setup...**

2 Select the **Sheet** tab.

3 Specify the rows and/or columns that you want to repeat.

4 Move the **Page Setup** dialog box so you can see the rows/columns, and drag over the row numbers or column letters.

5 Click **OK**.

## Headers and footers

Headers and footers display information at the top or bottom of every page that prints out for your worksheet. They are useful for page numbers, your name, the date that the worksheet is printed, the worksheet name, the workbook name – or any other information that you would like to appear in them.

**To add a header and/or footer to your pages:**

1 Open the **Page Setup** dialog box.

2 Select the **Header/Footer** tab.

Specify Custom

Click to display options

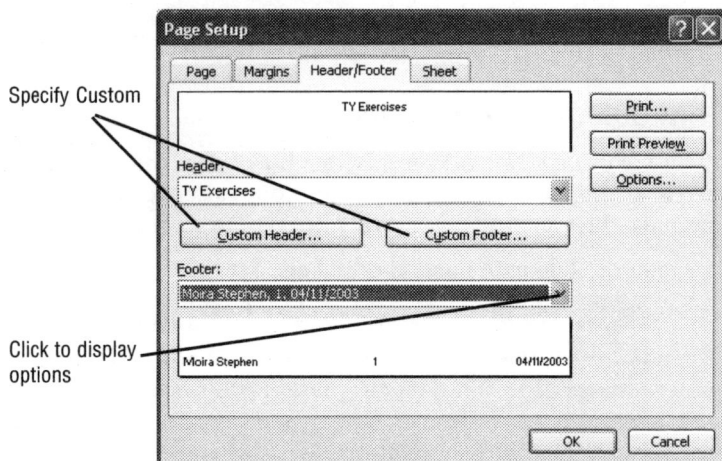

3 Choose a header or footer from the list of options.

4 Click **OK**.

You don't need to use one of the options listed. You can set up any header or footer you want.

**To set a custom Header or Footer:**

1 Select the **Header/Footer** tab in the **Page Setup** dialog box.

2 Click **Custom Header...** or **Custom Footer...**

Total no. of pages     Time printed     File     Insert picture

Page no.     Date printed     Folder     Sheet

Font     Format Painter

Footer

To format text, select the text, then choose the font button.
To insert a page number, date, time, file path, filename, or tab name: position the
insertion point in the edit box, then choose the appropriate button.
To insert picture: press the Insert Picture button. To format your picture, place the
cursor in the edit box and press the Format Picture button.

OK

Cancel

A

Left section:          Center section:          Right section:

Moira Stephen          &[Page]          &[Date]

Inserts date when printed

**3** Click in the section you want your header or footer to appear in – left, centre or right.

**4** Type in the text you want to appear in the header or footer.

Or

♦ Click the appropriate button to add page numbers, date, time, filepath (folder), file or sheet name, or a picture, or to use the Format Painter.

**5** Click **OK**.

## Gridlines, row and column headings

When you print your worksheet out, the gridlines, row and column headings do not print. This is usually how you would want it, but there may be times when it is useful to print out the gridlines and/or the row and column headings – for example, when printing out the formulas and functions you have used (see Chapter 5).

You can specify that you want the gridlines, row and column headings to print in the **Page Setup** dialog box.

**1** Open the **File** menu and choose **Page Setup**, then select the **Sheet** tab.

**2** In the Print options, select the **Gridlines** and/or the **Row and column headings** checkboxes as required.

**3** Click **OK**.

## Page order

If your worksheet is going to print out on more than one sheet of paper, the pages can be printed **down then over** or **over then down**. You can specify the order you prefer.

**1** Open the **Page Setup** dialog box and select the **Sheet** tab.

**2** In the **Page order** options, select the order required.

**3** Click **OK**.

### Summary

In this chapter we have discussed:

- Bold, italic and underline

- Alignment options – left, right, center, merge and center

- Font, font size, font colour, background colour, cell borders in individual cells or ranges on the worksheet

- The Format Painter

- Conditional formatting

- Changing the default font

- Keeping column headings and row labels displayed by freezing panes

- Viewing different parts of a worksheet at the same time by splitting the screen

- Page layout options

# 04

## working with sheets

**In this chapter you will learn:**

- about worksheet layout
- how to insert, delete and rename worksheets
- about moving and copying worksheets
- how to group worksheets
- to change the tab colour

## Aims of this chapter

This chapter discusses some options you will find useful when working with worksheets, and also looks at designing a worksheet. You will learn how to add worksheets to a workbook, delete, rename, copy and move them. You will also find out how to group worksheets and enter data, text or formulas on several worksheets simultaneously.

# 4.1 Moving between worksheets

The worksheet tabs appear at the bottom left of your screen – to the left of the horizontal scrollbar.

**To move from one sheet to another in your workbook:**

- Click the sheet tab of the sheet you want to work on.

If you can't see all the sheet tabs in the sheet tab bar, you can use the buttons to the left to scroll the sheet tabs into view.

Scroll sheet tabs    Sheet tabs    Tab split box

You can change the amount of space allocated to the sheet tab bar and the horizontal scroll bar by dragging the Tab split box between the sheet tabs and the horizontal scroll bar.

# 4.2 Worksheet design

Before you start setting up a worksheet, you should give some thought to its design. The main areas to keep in mind are:

- The purpose of your worksheet – ask yourself:
  - What do you want to communicate?
  - What should be emphasized or de-emphasized?
  - How will you show the relationship between areas?
- Keep it simple.

- Be consistent – within and across worksheets. If you produce the same worksheet every month, regular readers will be able to find the information they need quickly if it's always in the same place.

- Use formatting and layout options to add contrast to different areas of your worksheet.

There are no hard and fast rules – the main aim is to display the data in a clear and unambiguous way. If you like your worksheet layout and your audience can understand it, it's probably okay.

## Some Do's and Don't's of worksheet design

**Do** use fonts that are easy to read – Arial (the default) is a very 'clean' font, Times New Roman is easy on the eye.

**Do** make use of 'white space' – leave blank rows or columns between sections of your worksheet to make it easier to read.

**Do** use borders and/or shading to divide large sheets into manageable chunks and to draw attention to subtotals and totals.

**Do** format your numbers appropriately – currency, number of decimal places, percentage, etc.

**Do** make sure your worksheet is legible – don't use too small a font size or shrink to fit data to the extent it is too small to read.

**Do** add comments to cells that need an explanation.

**Don't** use too many different fonts or font sizes on a worksheet.

**Don't** overdo font and fill colours – you'll give your readers a headache!

**Don't** print gridlines out on a final report – they will give it a very cluttered look, though they may be useful on a draft printout, or one with formulas displayed.

# 4.3 Inserting worksheets

When you create a workbook in Excel the default number of worksheets is three. This may be enough (or more than enough), but if you need more than three in a workbook you can easily add them.

**To insert a worksheet:**

**1** Select a worksheet (click on the sheet tab).

**2** Open the **Insert** menu and choose **Worksheet**.

Or

**1** Right-click on a tab.

**2** Choose **Insert** from the shortcut menu.

**3** Select the **General** tab in the **Insert** dialog box.

**4** Choose **Worksheet** and click **OK**.

◆ The worksheet will be inserted to the left of the selected one, but can be moved as required (see section 4.6).

## Default sheets in a workbook

If you need to add new worksheets to most of your workbooks, you could change the default number of sheets in a new work-book to save you always having to add more.

**To change the default number of sheets:**

**1** Open the **Tools** menu and choose **Options**.

**2** Select the **General** tab.

**3** Set the number of sheets you require in the **Sheets in new workbook:** field.

**4** Click **OK**.

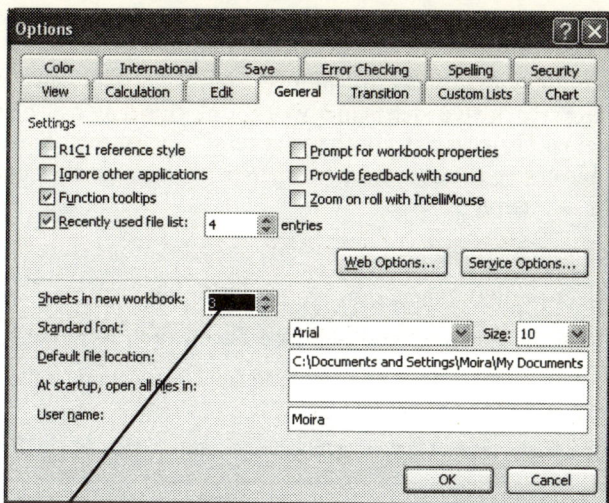

Default number of sheets

# 4.4 Deleting worksheets

If a workbook has too many sheets you can delete any you don't
need.

**To delete a worksheet:**

**1** Click on its tab to select the sheet you want to delete.

**2** Open the **Edit** menu and choose **Delete Sheet**.

Or

**1** Right-click on the sheet tab of the sheet you want to delete.

**2** Select **Delete** from the shortcut menu.

♦ If the sheet contains data, you will be asked to confirm the
deletion.

**3** Respond to the prompt – click **Delete** if you really want to
delete the sheet, **Cancel** if you change your mind.

Be careful when deleting worksheets – **Undo** will not restore
them!

# 4.5 Renaming worksheets

By default, worksheets are named *Sheet1*, *Sheet2*, etc. If you only use one or two sheets in a workbook this may cause you no problems. However, if you have several worksheets, life would be a bit easier if you renamed them with a name that actually meant something.

**To rename a worksheet:**

**1** Select the worksheet you want to rename.

**2** Open the **Format** menu, choose **Sheet**, then **Rename**.

**3** The sheet tab name will become selected – type in the name you want to use.

| ◄ ◄ ► ► ◄ ╱ Sheet2 ╱ Sales Figures ╲ Screen the Nut ╱ | ◄ | ► |
| Ready | | NUM |

**4** Press [**Enter**] or click anywhere on the worksheet.

Or

**1** Double-click on the sheet tab you want to rename.

**2** Type in the name you want to use.

**3** Press [**Enter**] or click anywhere on the worksheet.

# 4.6 Moving and copying worksheets

If you want to change the position of a worksheet within your workbook, you can move it to the position required. You can also move a worksheet to a new workbook or to another open workbook.

**To move a worksheet:**

**1** Select the sheet to move or copy.

**2** Open the **Edit** menu and choose **Move or Copy Sheet...**

**3** Choose the book to move or copy the sheet to in the **To book:** field.

**4** Select a sheet – this doesn't apply if you choose *New book* in the **To book:** field.

**Move or Copy** ✕

Move selected sheets
To book:

TY Exercises.xls ▾

Before sheet:

Simon's Sports
Sheet2
Sales Figures
Screw the Nut
(move to end)

☐ Create a copy

OK | Cancel

**5** Select **Create a copy** if you want to make a copy of the sheet rather than move it.

**6** Click **OK** – the sheet will be inserted before the one you selected.

♦ If you move or copy your worksheet to a new book, remember to save the new workbook if you want to keep it.

You can also move or copy worksheets within a workbook by dragging the worksheet tab to the position required.

**To move the worksheet:**

♦ Click and drag the worksheet tab of the sheet you want to move along the sheet tabs until it is in the correct place.

**To copy the worksheet:**

♦ Click on the worksheet tab, hold down [Ctr*l*] and drag the tab to the required position. The name will have (2) after it, to show that the new sheet is a copy – edit this as required.

# 4.7 Grouping worksheets

There may be times when you want to enter the same text, data or formulas into corresponding cells in more than one worksheet.

You could enter your work onto one worksheet, then copy it onto the others, or you could group the worksheets together and enter the standard text, data, formulas and/or functions and formatting that will appear on them all.

When worksheets are grouped, anything you do on one sheet is automatically replicated on every worksheet in the group.

**To gro*u*p adjacent worksheets:**

**1** Click on the sheet tab of the first sheet you want in the group.

**2** Hold down [**Shift**] and click on the last sheet tab you want in the group.

**To gro*u*p non-adjacent worksheets:**

**1** Click on the sheet tab of the first sheet in the group.

**2** Hold down [Ctr*l*] and click on each sheet tab that you want in the group.

When worksheets are grouped the word [**Group**] appears on the workbook Title bar.

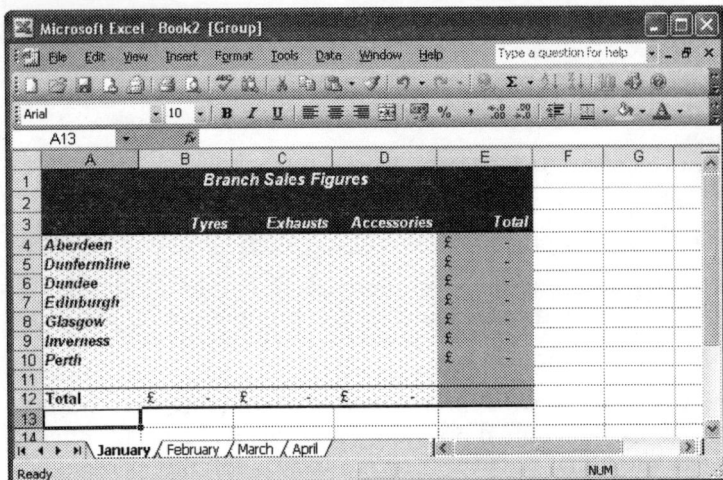

## To ungroup worksheets:

*   Click on any worksheet tab that isn't part of the group.

Or

1   Right-click on one of the grouped worksheet tabs.

2   Choose **Ungroup Sheets** from the pop-up menu.

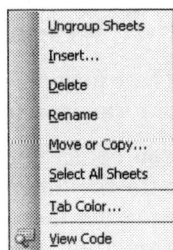

Ungroup Sheets

Insert...

Delete

Rename

Move or Copy...

Select All Sheets

Tab Color...

View Code

## Colour coding

If you have several worksheets in a book (or related sheets across books) you may find colouring the sheet tabs to be useful.

## To change the tab colour:

1   Select the tab(s).

2   Right-click on the tabs and choose **Tab Color...**

3   Select a colour.

4   Click **OK**.

Format Tab Color

Tab Color

No Color

OK      Cancel

## Summary

In this chapter we have discussed:

- Moving between sheets in a workbook
- Things to consider when designing a worksheet layout
- Inserting sheets into a workbook
- Changing the default number of sheets in a workbook
- Deleting sheets from a workbook
- Renaming sheets
- Moving and copying sheets within a workbook
- Moving and copying sheets to a new workbook
- Grouping worksheets
- Changing the tab colour

# 05

## formulas and functions

**In this chapter you will learn:**

- more about functions and formulas
- about relative and absolute addresses and circular references
- how to use named ranges
- how to add comments and protect your worksheet

## Aims of this chapter

This chapter continues our discussions of formulas and introduces some of the many Excel functions that you might find useful. We will discuss AutoSum, statistical functions, named ranges, cell comments and worksheet protection.

# 5.1 AutoSum

The worksheet below contains details of quarterly sales figures. Enter the text and data into a new worksheet in your workbook. We need to calculate the total sales figures for each sales representative for the year and also the total sales for each quarter.

You could use a formula to calculate the total (e.g. in F4 you might have =B4+C4+D4+E4), but the easist and quickest way to calculate it is with AutoSum.

To calculate the totals using AutoSum:

1  Select a cell in which you want a total figure to appear, e.g. the cell that will contain the total sales for the first sales person or the total for Quarter 1.

2  Click the **AutoSum** tool $\Sigma$ on the Standard toolbar.

**3** The range of cells to be added together will be highlighted. Note that the function also appears in the formula bar.

**4** If the suggested range of cells is correct, press [**Enter**].

• If the suggested range is *not* the range of cells you want to add, drag over the correct range, then press [**Enter**].

The total value of the selected range will appear in the active cell when you accept the formula by pressing [**Enter**].

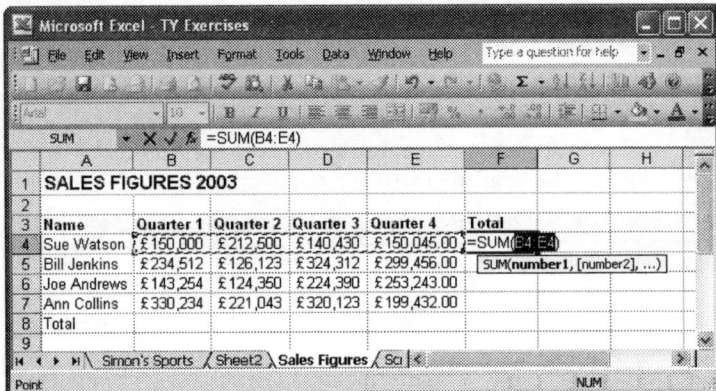

• Excel calculates the total of the selected cells using the SUM function. Its syntax is =**SUM(cell range)** – you can type in the function, but it's easier (and less error prone) to use AutoSum.

You could select each of the total cells in turn and use AutoSum to calculate their totals, or use AutoFill (see section 2.11) to copy the function down or across the other total cells.

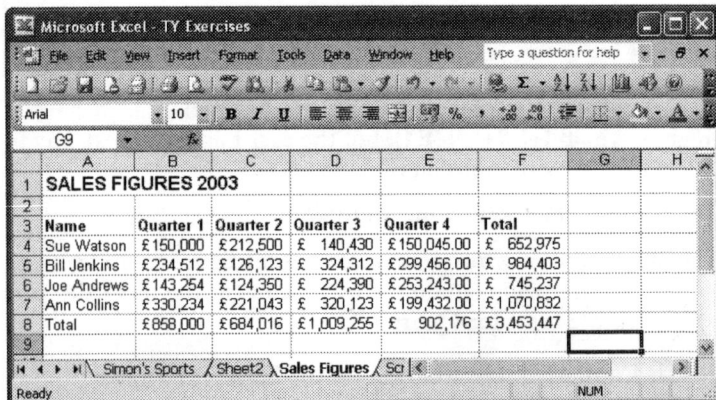

If you are totalling rows and columns as in this example, you could use a shortcut that performs all the calculations in one move.

## To AutoSum several groups of cells simultaneously:

**1** Select all of the rows and columns to total, and the cells to contain the results of the AutoSum calculations.

**2** Click the **AutoSum** tool [Σ] on the Standard toolbar.

The cells in the rightmost column and bottom row of the selected area will each have the Sum function inserted into them.

## Non-adjacent cells

You can also use AutoSum to total non-adjacent cells if you wish.

## To total non-adjacent cells:

**1** Select the cell that will contain the result of the calculation.

**2** Click the **AutoSum** tool [Σ] on the Standard toolbar.

**3** Click on the first cell you want to include in the range.

**4** Hold down [**Ctrl**] and click on each of the other cells to be included in the function.

**5** Press [**Enter**].

- If you prefer to type in the function, you must start with = (equals sign). A range of adjacent cells has the first cell address in the range entered, followed by : (colon), then the last cell address in the range. The cell addresses for non-adjacent cells must be separated by , (comma).

### Excel functions

Excel has many functions that you can use on your data. There are statistical, financial, logical, text, database, lookup, data and time functions, etc. It is very unlikely that you will need to use them all (you'll be glad to know!), but we'll look at some that are useful at a general level. You can then go on and explore the functions and find any that may be useful in your particular situation. Use the online Help as necessary.

## 5.2 Common statistical functions

The most commonly used statistical functions – average, count, maximum and minimum – can all be found in the AutoSum list.

| | |
|---|---|
| MIN | returns the smallest value |
| MAX | returns the highest value |
| AVERAGE | returns the mean value (=total/count) |
| COUNT | returns the number of numeric entries |

There are lots of other statistical functions in the **Insert Function** dialog box (see section 5.3). You can display the box by clicking **More Functions...** at the bottom of the AutoSum list.

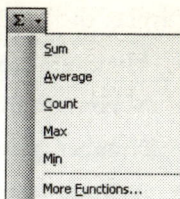

A useful statistical function not on the AutoSum list is **Counta**, which returns the number of numeric and text entries.

The Average, Count, Counta, Min and Max work in exactly the same way as the Sum function in the AutoSum list.

1 Select the cell that the result will be displayed in.

2 Choose the function required from the AutoSum list.

3 Drag over (or [**Ctrl**]-click) to select the cells that the function will use.

4 Press [**Enter**].

♦ Try them out on your Simon's Sports data.

| Item | Code | Rec Retail Price | Sale Price | Saving |
|---|---|---|---|---|
| **Simon's Sports** | | | | |
| *End of Season Sale - everything must go!* | | | | |
| | | | | |
| Holdall (black) | H123 | £15.50 | £9.99 | £5.51 |
| Rucksack | R12 | £16.99 | £9.99 | £7.00 |
| Badminton Racket | B25 | £24.00 | £15.99 | £8.01 |
| Squash Racket | S44-A | £27.75 | £19.99 | £7.76 |
| Hockey Stick | H220 | £16.99 | 9.99 | £7.00 |
| Rucksack | R15 | £40.00 | £29.99 | £10.01 |
| Hockey Stick | H221 | £18.88 | £10.99 | £7.89 |
| Dumbell Set | D12 | £36.99 | £24.00 | £12.99 |
| Home Gym | HG3 | £245.99 | £175.00 | £70.99 |
| Tennis Racket | T101 | £35.99 | £25.99 | £10.00 |
| Rucksack | R10 | £7.99 | £5.49 | £2.50 |
| | | | | |
| Minimum saving | £2.50 | | | |
| Maximum saving | £70.99 | | | |
| Number of items for sale | 11 | | | |
| Average sale price | £30.67 | | | |

Display these values:

- **Minimum** from the saving column.
- **Maximum** from the saving column.
- **Number** of items on sale.
- **Average** sale price of the items in the list.

## 5.3 The Insert Function dialog box

To insert a function:

1 Select the cell that you want the function to go in.

2 Click the **Function** button [_fx_] (to the left of the Formula bar).

- The **Insert Function** dialog box is displayed.

**Search for a function:**

1 Type what you want to do in the **Search for a function** field.

2 Click **Go**.

- Excel will display a list of functions that it thinks might help.

3 Scroll through the list to see what's there.

4 Select the function and click **OK**.

**Selecting a function (without searching):**

1 Select the category that your function is in (choose **All** if you're not sure which category).

**2** Scroll through the list until you find the function you need.

**3** Select it and click **OK**.

♦ You can get help on any function from this dialog box if you select it and click **Help on this function**.

Once you've selected a function the **Function Arguments** dialog box appears.

Minimize the dialog box to change the selected cells

| Function Arguments | | | × |
|---|---|---|---|
| MAX | | | |
| Number1 | D5:D15 | ▦ | = {9.99;9.99;15.99;19 |
| Number2 | | ▦ | = number |

= 175

Returns the largest value in a set of values. Ignores logical values and text.

**Number1:** number1,number2,... are 1 to 30 numbers, empty cells, logical values, or text numbers for which you want the maximum.

Formula result = 175

Help on this function | OK | Cancel |

♦ If the **Function Arguments** dialog box obscures the area of the worksheet you want to view, click the ▦ button to the right of a data entry field – it will become minimized, so you can see your worksheet.

♦ To display the dialog box again, click the restore button at the far right of the minimized window.

| Function Arguments | × |
|---|---|
| D5:D15 | ▣ |

— Restore

♦ The **More Functions...** option at the end of the AutoSum list or the Functions list opens the **Insert Function** dialog box.

**To edit a function:**

**1** Select the cell that contains the function.

**2** Edit the function in the formula bar.

Or

♦ Click the **Insert Function** button again to display the **Function Arguments** dialog box.

### Recently used functions list

You can quickly add any recently used function to the Formula bar using the Function list. The list displays the recently used functions.

**1** Select the cell where you want the function to go.

**2** Type '='.

**3** The **Name** box changes to a Function list.

**4** Click the drop-down arrow to the right of the list.

**5** Select the function required.

**6** Complete the **Function Arguments** dialog box as required.

**7** Click **OK**.

◆ **More Functions...** at the bottom of the list opens the **Insert Function** dialog box.

## 5.4 View formulas

When setting up your worksheet, it is sometimes useful to display and print the formulas and functions that you have entered into the cells.

Each formula or function is displayed in the formula bar when its cell is selected, but you can get Excel to display all the formulas and functions in your worksheet if you wish.

**To display the formulas and functions:**

**1** Open the **Tools** menu and choose **Options...**

**2** Select the **View** tab.

**3** Select the **Formulas** checkbox and click **OK**.

◆ The keyboard shortcut [**Ctrl**] – [ | ] (at the far left above [**Tab**]) toggles the display of formulas.

You may need to adjust the column widths to display the whole formula or function in some columns.

◆ You can print a copy of your worksheet out with the formulas and functions displayed – a printout is often useful for reference purposes.

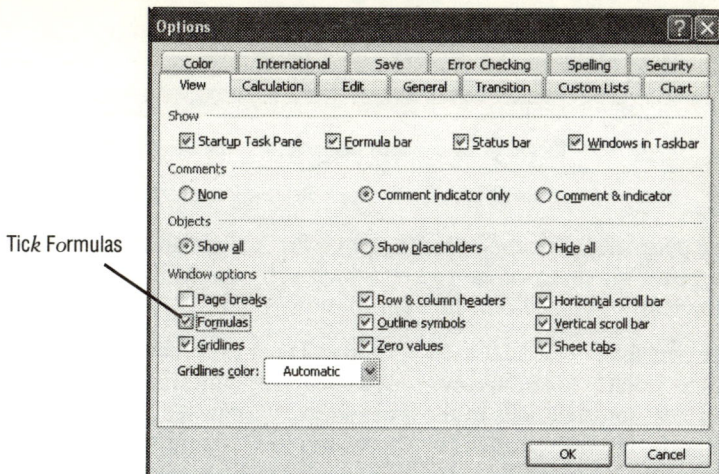

Tick Formulas

The formulas and functions used in the Simon's Sports worksheet are displayed below – note that what you can see is the data exactly as it was entered, and not as it is displayed on screen.

**Simon's Sports**
*End of Season Sale - everything must go!*

| Item | Code | Rec Retail Price | Sale Price | Saving |
|------|------|-------|------------|--------|
| Holdall (black) | H123 | 15.5 | 9.99 | =C5-D5 |
| Rucksack | R12 | 16.99 | 9.99 | =C6-D6 |
| Badminton Racket | B25 | 24 | 15.99 | =C7-D7 |
| Squash Racket | S44-A | 27.75 | 19.99 | =C8-D8 |
| Hockey Stick | H220 | 16.99 | 9.99 | =C9-D9 |
| Rucksack | R15 | 40 | 29.99 | =C10-D10 |
| Hockey Stick | H221 | 18.88 | 10.99 | =C11-D11 |
| Dumbell Set | D12 | 36.99 | 24 | =C12-D12 |
| Home Gym | HG3 | 245.99 | 175 | =C13-D13 |
| Tennis Racket | T101 | 35.99 | 25.99 | =C14-D14 |
| Rucksack | R10 | 7.99 | 5.49 | =C15-D15 |

| | |
|---|---|
| Minimum saving | =MIN(E5:E15) |
| Maximum saving | =MAX(E5:E15) |
| Number of items for sale | =COUNTA(A5:A15) |
| Average sale price | =AVERAGE(D5:D15) |

The **Formula Auditing** toolbar appears when your formulas are displayed. You can use this toolbar to identify which cells are dependent on others, and which cell values are precedents – i.e. have values that are referred to in formulas in other cells.

**The Formula Auditing toolbar**

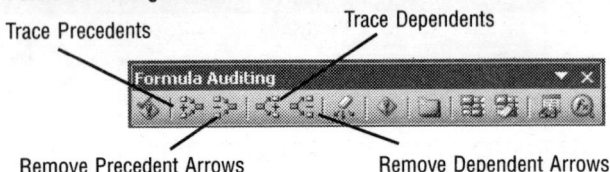

Trace Precedents        Trace Dependents

Remove Precedent Arrows        Remove Dependent Arrows

Experiment with the Trace/Remove Precedents and Dependents arrows on the toolbar to see which cells are influenced by, or have an influence on, the values in other cells.

If you select cell E10 then click the **Trace Precedents** and **Trace Dependents** tools, arrows will appear showing the relationship of E10 to other cells in the worksheet. We can see that the value in cell E10 is dependent on the values in C10 and D10, and that those in B17 and B18 are influenced by the value in E10. This graphical representation of the relationship between cells can be useful when you need to check what is going on in a worksheet. You can remove the arrows selectively using **Remove Precedent Arrows** and **Remove Dependent Arrows** as required, or click **Remove All Arrows**.

• To hide the formulas again, go to the **View** tab in the **Options** dialog box, clear the **Formulas** checkbox and click **OK**. or press [**Ctrl**]-[**I**].

# 5.5 Relative and absolute addresses

You have already noticed that when you AutoFill or copy a formula, the cell addresses used in it change automatically, relative to the position you copy them to. By default, cell addresses are *relative*. There will be times when you use a cell address in a formula, and want to copy it into other cells, but don't want the address to change relative to its position.

In the next example, we are going to calculate the income from admissions to a film centre.

• Enter the data onto a new worksheet (see section 4.3 if you need to add a new sheet). DO NOT complete the Revenue columns – we will enter formulas to calculate the figures.

To calculate the January revenue figures:

**1** Enter a formula into the *Adult* cell in the *January, Revenue* column to calculate the income from this group. The first revenue figure for January is calculated by multiplying the

number of adults (B11) by the adult admission rate (D5).
The formula in C11 should be **=B11*D5**.

**2** Use AutoFill (see section 2.11) to copy the formula down
over the *OAP* and *Concession* cells.

We could enter the appropriate formulas into the February and
March columns in a similar way. However, it would be quicker to
*copy* the January formulas. This poses two possible problems:

- We don't want the D5 (adult rate), D6 (OAP rate), D7 (concession rate) addresses to change when we copy the formula.

- We can't use AutoFill because the cells we want to copy to
  are not next to the source cells.

To stop the cell addresses from changing when we copy them,
we must create *absolute addresses*. An absolute address will not
change when the formula containing it is copied or moved.

An absolute cell address is marked by a $ sign in front of each
coordinate that must not change.

You can type the $ sign, or use [**F4**] on your keyboard.

**To absolutely address the cells in a formula:**

**1** Select the cell that contains the formula (C11, C12 or C13 in
this example) – the formula appears in the Formula bar.

**2** Click in the Formula bar.

**3** Place the insertion point to the *right* of the cell address you
want to make absolute (D5 or D6 or D7).

**4** Press [**F4**] until you have the cell addressed properly.

> ▨ **=** =B11*$D$5

- Each time you press [**F4**] it moves through the absolute ad-
  dressing options.

| $D$5 | neither coordinate will change |
|------|--------------------------------|
| D$5  | the column will change if you copy the formula across columns |
| $D5  | the row number will change if you copy the formula down rows |
| D5   | both coordinates will change relative to its new position |

Absolutely address the admission rate cell address in each of the January formula – either $D$5 or $D5 will do. We will later copy the formula across the columns, but must look back to column D for our data.

Once you've made the appropriate cell addresses absolute, you can copy the formula across to the February and March columns.

### To complete the February and March figures:

1 Select the cells you are copying from – the *January, Revenue* figures in this case, C11:C13.

2 Click the **Copy** tool on the Standard toolbar.

3 Select the first cell you want to paste into e.g. E11 for the *February* figures – you don't need to select E11:E13.

4 Click the **Paste** tool on the Standard toolbar.

5 Select cell G11 as the first cell for the *March* figures.

6 Click the **Paste** tool on the Standard toolbar.

7 Press [Esc] on your keyboard to cancel the copy routine.

Your final worksheet should look similar to the ones shown. The first picture displays the formulas (you may have different cell addresses if you have used different rows and columns for your data), the second one shows the results.

Screenshot of Microsoft Excel - TY Exercises showing:

| | A | B | C | D | E | F | G |
|---|---|---|---|---|---|---|---|
| 1 | | | SOUTHSIDE FILM CENTRE | | | | |
| 2 | | | MONTHLY TAKINGS FROM ADMISSIONS | | | | |
| 3 | | | | | | | |
| 4 | | | Admission Charges | | | | |
| 5 | | | Adult | £ 4.00 | | | |
| 6 | | | OAP | £ 2.50 | | | |
| 7 | | | Concession | £ 2.00 | | | |
| 8 | | | | | | | |
| 9 | | | January | | February | | March |
| 10 | | | Number | Revenue | Number | Revenue | Number | Revenue |
| 11 | Adult | | 2345 | £ 9,380.00 | 2789 | £11,156.00 | 3105 | £12,420.00 |
| 12 | OAP | | 1750 | £ 4,375.00 | 1900 | £ 4,750.00 | 2100 | £ 5,250.00 |
| 13 | Concession | | 4321 | £ 8,642.00 | 4750 | £ 9,500.00 | 5125 | £10,250.00 |

## 5.6 Circular references

If you create a formula that refers to its own cell, you have a *circular reference*. Excel cannot resolve these using normal calculation methods and a warning will appear should one occur.

Microsoft Excel dialog: Microsoft Office Excel cannot calculate a formula. Cell references in the formula refer to the formula's result, creating a circular reference. Try one of the following:
• If you accidentally created the circular reference, click OK. This will display the Circular Reference toolbar and help for using it to correct your formula.
• For more information about circular references and how to work with them, click Help.
• To continue leaving the formula as it is, click Cancel.

[OK] [Cancel] [Help]

Click OK and read the Help page that appears, and minimize it so that you can refer back to it quickly if necessary.

♦ The Circular Reference toolbar has **Trace Precedents, Trace Dependents** and **Remove All Arrows** tools (similar to the Formula Auditing toolbar – see section 5.4) so that you can display the arrows to help you work out what is going on.

**To review and amend circular references:**

**1** Go to the first cell that is registering a circular reference – use the **Navigate Circular Reference** box on the toolbar.

**2** Study the formula or function – if you spot the error, amend as necessary.

```
Microsoft Excel - TY Exercises
 File  Edit  View  Insert  Format  Tools  Data  Window  Help

Arial            10    B  I  U
      F4              =SUM(B4:F4)
        A         B         C         D         E         F         G
1  SALES FIGURES 2003
2
3  Name       Quarter 1  Quarter 2  Quarter 3  Quarter 4   Total
4  Sue Watson £ 150,000  £ 212,500  £   140,430  £ 150,045.00  £      -
5  Bill Jenkins £ 234,512  £ 126,123  £   324,312  £ 299,456.00  £   984,403
6  Joe Andrews £ 143,254  £ 124,350  £   224,390  £ 253,243.00  £   745,237
7  Ann Collins £ 330,234  £ 221,043  £   320,123  £ 199,432.00  £ 1,070,832
8  Total      £ 858,000  £ 684,016  £ 1,009,255  £   902,176  £ 3,453,447
9
10
11                        Circular Reference
12                        $F$4
13
14
   Simon's Sports \ Sales Figures / Scr
Ready                      Circular: F4                              NUM
```

**3** If you can't see what is wrong, try the next cell that is causing a problem (click the drop-down arrow on the **Navigate Circular Reference** box).

**4** Review and edit the cells as necessary, until you have solved the problem.

♦ When the circular reference problem is resolved, the Circular Reference toolbar will disappear.

♦ Note that the status bar says 'Circular', with the address of the cell that is causing the problem, when a circular reference is present. This will disappear when you have solved the problem. If no cell address is present, the *active* worksheet does not contain the circular reference.

Some engineering and scientific formulas require circular references – in this case you may need to change the number of iterations (the number of times Excel recalculates the sheet).

**To change the number of iterations:**

**1** Choose **Options** from the **Tools** menu.

**2** On the **Calculation** tab, select the **Iteration** checkbox then specify the maximum number of iterations and degree of change you want Excel to use.

# 5.7 Named ranges

When building up your formulas and functions, you have been using cell addresses to tell Excel which cells you want to use in your calculations. Cell addresses are not really very user-friendly – it isn't always immediately clear what the formula =B13*$B$6 or the function =AVERAGE(D5:D17) is actually doing.

To make your worksheet easier to understand you can use *named ranges* instead of cell addresses in your formulas and functions.

There are two main ways of naming ranges.

* Use the existing labels that are on your worksheet to refer to the related data.

Or

* Create new descriptive names.

## Create named ranges

You can easily give a cell or range of cells a name. The name used can be anything you like (as long as it obeys the rules below) or you can use column and/or row labels as names for your cell ranges. Named ranges that you create are available to any worksheet within the workbook.

*Rules for naming ranges:*

* The maximum size for a name is 255 characters.

* Spaces are not allowed (use an underline or a full stop to separate words).

* The first character in a name *must* be a letter or an underline character (other characters can be letters, numbers, full stops and underlines, but not commas, question marks or other punctuation characters).

* You *cannot* use a cell reference for a range name, e.g. B75 or AA$24.

* Names can contain upper and lower case letters. Excel is *not* case sensitive. If you create a name called *Profit*, then another called *PROFIT*, the second will replace the first.

**To name a cell, or range of cells, within a worksheet:**

**1** Select the cell or range of cells you want to name.

**2** Click the **Name** box at the left edge of the Formula bar.

**3** Type in a name for the cells.

**4** Press [**Enter**].

Name box

You could name the ranges for the admission charges in the Film Centre worksheet, with names such as *Adult_rate*, *OAP_rate* and *Con_rate*.

**To name cells using the existing row and column headings:**

**1** Select the cells you want to name – including the row and/or column headings.

**2** Open the **Insert** menu and choose **Name**, then **Create**.

**3** In the **Create Names** dialog box, select the location that contains the labels by ticking the appropriate checkbox(es).

**4** Click **OK**.

You could create named ranges for the columns in the *Screw the Nut plc* worksheet using this method.

You can easily paste range names into your formula or function, rather than using the cell addresses.

**To use a range name in a formula or function:**

**1** Select the cell that will contain your formula.

**2** Enter the formula as normal *until* you want to refer to a named range.

**3** Open the **Insert** menu, choose **Name** then **Paste**.

**4** Select the name you want to paste, then click **OK**.

| Paste Name | ✕ |
|---|---|
| Paste name | |
| Adult_rate | |
| Con_rate | |
| Cost_retail | |
| Cost_trade | |
| Number_in_Stock | |
| OAP_rate | |
| Profit | |
| Value_of_Stock | |
| OK | Cancel |

**5** Continue writing the formula.

If you no longer use a range name, you can delete it. Deleting the range name *does not* delete the cell contents, but it will affect any cells that refer to the named range in a formula.

**To delete a range name:**

**1** Open the **Insert** menu and choose **Name**, then **Define**.

**2** Select the range name you want to delete.

**3** Click **Delete** and close the **Define Name** dialog box.

• The error message **#NAME?** appears in a cell that refers to a named range that does not exist.

## Converting cell addresses to named ranges

If you find that you prefer using named ranges to cell addresses in your worksheets, but you have already created formulas using cell addresses, you can easily convert these cell addresses to named ranges for all or part of your worksheet. Create names for the ranges of cells that you want to convert – see above.

**1** To convert all of the cell addresses in your formulas to named ranges, select any single cell in your worksheet.

Or

• To convert only part of your worksheet, select the range of cells required.

**2** Open the **Insert** menu, choose **Name** then **Apply**.

**3** Select the names you want to apply from the **Apply names list**.

**4** Click **OK**.

The **Apply Names** dialog:

Apply names:
Adult_rate
Con_rate
Cost__retail
Cost__trade
Number_in_Stock
OAP_rate
Profit
Value_of_Stock

OK
Cancel
Options >>

☑ Ignore Relative/Absolute
☑ Use row and column names

• If you have created named ranges for the columns in the *Screw the Nut plc* worksheet, try converting the formulas using this method.

• The cell addresses in the formulas will have been replaced by the range names.

The *Screw the Nut plc* worksheet is displayed below. The cell addresses originally used in the formulas were converted to the named ranges using the method described above.

SCREW T

Stock Valu

| Part No | Description | Cost (trade) | Cost (retail) | Profit | Number in Stock | Value of Stock |
|---|---|---|---|---|---|---|
| S1113 | Screwdriver set | 10 | 18.99 | =Cost__retail-Cost__trade | 4 | =Cost__trade*Number_in_Stock |
| S2451 | Spanner set | 14 | 20.99 | =Cost__retail-Cost__trade | 6 | =Cost__trade*Number_in_Stock |
| W2201 | Wrench & Grip set | 9 | 15.99 | =Cost__retail-Cost__trade | 6 | =Cost__trade*Number_in_Stock |
| W3120 | Workman (B&D) | 60 | 75 | =Cost__retail-Cost__trade | 3 | =Cost__trade*Number_in_Stock |
| | | | | Total value of stock | | =SUM(Value_of_Stock) |

## 5.8 Comments

If you think that the purpose of a formula in a cell is not self-explicit, you can add a *comment* to the cell. You will find them particularly useful if you don't use named ranges, and want to add an explanation, or, if others share your worksheets and you want to explain the logic behind an entry you have made.

**To add a comment to a cell:**

**1** Select the cell you want to add a comment to.

**2** Hold down [**Shift**] and press [**F2**].

Or

- Open the **Insert** menu and choose **Comment**.

**3** Type your comment into the box.

**4** Click outside the comment box.

If the comment remains on your screen, I suggest you change the comment view options to show only the comment indicator (a small red triangle).

**1** Open the **Tools** menu and choose **Options**.

**2** Select the **View** tab.

**3** In the **Comments** options, select **Comment indicator only**.

A small red triangle will appear in the top right corner of your cell to indicate it has a comment attached to it.

When you move your mouse pointer over the cell, the comment will be displayed.

**To edit a comment:**

**1** Select the cell that has the comment attached to it.

**2** Right-click on the cell and select **Edit Comment** from the shortcut menu that appears.

Or

The red triangle indicates the presence of
a comment – point to the cell to read it

* Hold down [**Shift**] and press [**F2**].

**3** Edit the comment as required.

**4** Click outside the comment box.

**To delete a comment:**

**1** Select the cell that has the comment attached to it.

**2** Right-click on the cell and select **Delete Comment** from the
shortcut menu that appears.

The **Reviewing** toolbar can be used to help you create, edit and
delete comments. To display the toolbar, choose **Toolbars** from
the **View** menu and select **Reviewing** from the list.

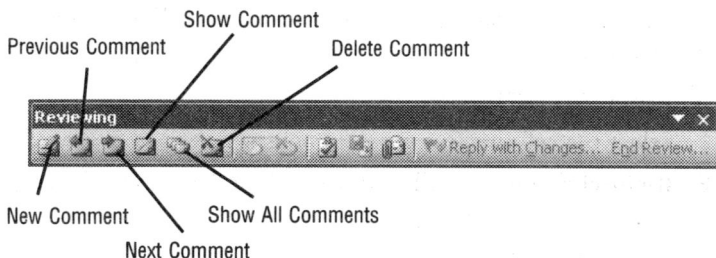

Previous Comment    Show Comment    Delete Comment

Reviewing

New Comment    Show All Comments
Next Comment

# 5.9 Worksheet protection

Having gone to the trouble of setting up formulas and functions on your worksheet, it would be a pity if they were accidentally overwritten when you are entering text and data. You can protect your worksheet to avoid this unfortunate situation arising.

When you protect a worksheet, cells formatted as *locked* cannot be edited, cells formatted as *unlocked* can. Initially all cells are locked. You must therefore unlock cells that you want to be able to edit in the protected sheet, before you turn on protection.

Once the worksheet has been protected, only those cells that you unlocked can be modified (unless you 'unprotect' the worksheet again).

**To identify the cells that are not to be locked:**

**1** Select the cells that you want unlocked.

**2** Open the **Format** menu and choose **Cells...**

**3** Select the **Protection** tab.

**4** Deselect the **Locked** checkbox.

**5** Click **OK**.

**To activate the protection:**

**1** On the **Tools** menu, point to **Protection** and select **Protect Sheet...**

**2** Tick the elements to protect.

**3** Set a password if you wish – just don't forget it!

**4** Re-enter the password at the prompt.

**5** Click **OK**.

To deactivate the protection:

**1** Open the **Tools** menu, point to **Protection** and select **Unprotect Sheet...** (or whatever option is appropriate).

**2** If you used a password, you'll be asked to enter it. Enter the password and click **OK**.

---

## Summary

In this chapter we have discussed:

- AutoSum and using the AutoSum list
- The Insert Function dialog box
- The Statistical functions MIN, MAX, AVERAGE, COUNT and COUNTA
- Viewing the formulas and functions in your worksheet
- Relative and absolute cell addresses
- Circular references
- Named ranges
- Adding comments to a cell
- Worksheet protection

# 06 more functions

**In this chapter you will learn:**

- about Logical, Statistical, Math, Text, Date and Financial functions
- how to use Lookup tables
- about Data Tables, Scenarios and PivotTables

## Aims of this chapter

In this chapter we will look at a number of functions from the different categories. Some logical, statistical, math, text, date, financial and lookup functions will be explored. Database functions will be considered in Chapter 9. We will also look at Data Tables, Scenarios and Pivot Tables.

# 6.1 Logical functions

## IF function

The IF function is used to return one value if the condition you specify is True, and another value if the condition is False. The values returned can be text, numbers, or the result of a formula or function.

For example, you might be entering student end-of-term exam results into your worksheet. If a student has 50% or more in the exam, a pass will be awarded, if less than 50% is achieved, the result is a fail.

| | A | B | C | D | E | F | G | H |
|---|---|---|---|---|---|---|---|---|
| 1 | END OF TERM EXAM RESULTS | | | | | | | |
| 2 | | | | | | | | |
| 3 | Firstname | Surname | Total Mark | Result | | | | |
| 4 | Gill | McLaren | 57 | | | | | |
| 5 | Peter | Shaw | 63 | | | | | |
| 6 | Kim | Stephen | 79 | | | | | |
| 7 | Andrew | Borthwick | 75 | | | | | |
| 8 | Alison | Peterson | 66 | | | | | |
| 9 | Amanda | Mitchell | 76 | | | | | |
| 10 | Gordon | Williamson | 38 | | | | | |
| 11 | Clare | Stephen | 83 | | | | | |
| 12 | Jack | Williamson | 77 | | | | | |
| 13 | Ann | Shaw | 42 | | | | | |
| 14 | | | | | | | | |
| 15 | | | | | | | | |

## Comparison operators

This example uses a comparison operator to check if the Total Mark is greater than or equal to 50. The operators include:

| | | | |
|---|---|---|---|
| = | equal to | <> | not equal to |
| > | greater than | >= | greater than or equal to |
| < | less than | <= | less than or equal to |

Enter the data on the previous page into a new worksheet.

To return a 'Pass' or 'Fail' message in the *Result* column, we need to enter the IF function.

You can use either cell addresses or named ranges in a function.

**To enter the function:**

**1** Select the first cell in the result column.

**2** Click the **Insert Function** button 𝑓ₓ to the left of the Formula bar.

**3** Select IF from the function list – you'll find it in the **Logical** category.

**4** Enter the condition that you want to be evaluated in the **Logical test** field *(Total_Mark>=50* in this case).

**5** Specify the value if the condition is found to be True – you don't need to type in the quotes – Excel will enter them automatically as it builds the formula.

**6** Specify the value if the condition is found to be False.

Function Arguments

IF

| Logical_test | Total_Mark>=50 | = {TRUE;TRUE;TRUE;1 |
| Value_if_true | "Pass" | = "Pass" |
| Value_if_false | Fail | = |

= {"Pass";"Pass";"Pass";"Pa

Checks whether a condition is met, and returns one value if TRUE, and another value if FALSE.

**Value_if_false** is the value that is returned if Logical_test is FALSE. If omitted, FALSE is returned.

Formula result =     Pass

Help on this function          OK     Cancel

**7** Click **OK**.

- AutoFill the function down through the Result column – Pass will appear in the rows where the condition is true, Fail will appear in the rows where the condition is false.

With the formulas displayed, the worksheet looks like the illustration below. This example uses named ranges rather than cell addresses. If we had used cell addresses the formulas would have been =IF(C4>=50, "Pass", "Fail"), etc.

## Nested IFs

The values used by functions to perform calculations or operations are called arguments. An argument may be a numeric value, a text value, a cell reference, a range of cells, a named range, or a nested function (a function within a function).

This next example illustrates nested IFs. We are going to add another column to our worksheet to give the Grade achieved by each student. We need to use the IF function to check the Total Mark and return the appropriate grade.

- IF a student gets 70% or more the grade is an A.
- IF the student gets 60% to 69% the grade is a B.
- IF the student gets 50% to 59% the grade is a C.
- Less than 50% is a fail.

As we have four possible outcomes this time (instead of a simple Pass or Fail) we must nest our IF functions to work through the various options.

- Add a new column heading, 'Grade', in the column to the right of the *Result* column.

1 Select the first cell in the *Grade* column.

2 Click the **Insert Function** button ![fx] and select IF from the function list.

3 Enter the condition that you want to be evaluated in the **Logical test** field (*Total_Mark>=70* in this case) and specify the **Value if true** – A (70% and over gets an A).

4 In the **Value if false** field, select IF again (from the function list to left of formula bar) – we need to check if a student has 60% or more. (This test will only be applied to students who *did not* get 70% or more.)

5 Complete the next set of conditions and values. Enter the condition that you want to be evaluated in the **Logical test** field (*Total_Mark>=60* in this case) and specify the **Value if true** – B (60% to 69% gets a B grade).

6 In the **Value if false** field select the IF function again – we need to check if the student has 50% or more (this test will only be applied to students who *did not* get 60–69%).

7 Enter the **Logical test** field data (*Total_Mark>=50* in this case).

**8** Specify the **Value if true** – C (50–59% gets a C grade) and the **Value if false** – Fail.

**9** Click **OK**.

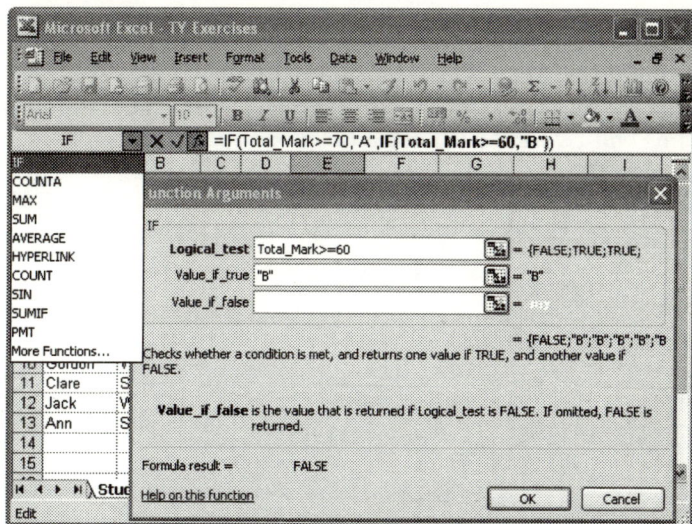

- AutoFill the functions down the column.

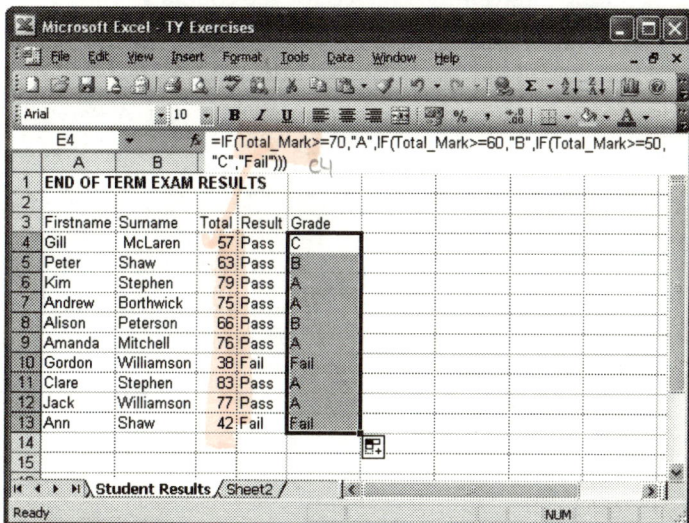

You should get A, B, C and Fail grades as appropriate. If the function does not work as expected, delete it and try again.

In this next example, the IF function is used to work out the amount of discount a customer will get on an order.

- If the order is £1,000 or over, 10% will be deducted.
- If the order is between £750 and £999, 5% will be deducted.
- If the order is less than £750, no discount is given.

Enter the basic worksheet as it is displayed here. The empty columns will be completed using functions and formulas.

Named ranges have been created for the columns.

- The Value of order column has been called *VOO*.
- The Discount column has been called *Discount*.
- The Net Amount column has been called *Net_Amount*.
- The VAT column has been called *VAT*.

These names have been used in the functions and formulas. The
formulas and functions required are displayed below.

| | A | B | C |
|---|---|---|---|
| 1 | Sales Orders | | |
| 2 | | | |
| 3 | Customer Code | Value of Order | Discount |
| 4 | ABC1 | 1523.75 | =IF(VOO>=1000,VOO*10%,IF(VOO>=750,VOO*5%,0)) |
| 5 | DEF2 | 890 | =IF(VOO>=1000,VOO*10%,IF(VOO>=750,VOO*5%,0)) |
| 6 | GHI3 | 600 | =IF(VOO>=1000,VOO*10%,IF(VOO>=750,VOO*5%,0)) |
| 7 | | | |
| 8 | | | |
| 9 | Net Amount | Vat | Total |
| 10 | =VOO-Discount | =Net_Amount*17.5% | =Net_Amount+Vat |
| 11 | =VOO-Discount | =Net_Amount*17.5% | =Net_Amount+Vat |
| 12 | =VOO-Discount | =Net_Amount*17.5% | =Net_Amount+Vat |
| 13 | | | |
| 14 | | | |

## AND

The AND function returns a TRUE result if all the conditions in
the function are met, and a FALSE result if all the conditions are
not met.

For example, you may manufacture and sell traditional children's
wooden toys. Your most popular items are a painted toy box, a
rocking horse and building blocks. You want to keep a record of
the items that customers buy from you.

| | A | B | C | D | E |
|---|---|---|---|---|---|
| 1 | Customer Purchase Data | | | | |
| 2 | Customer | Painted Toy Box | Rocking Horse | Building Blocks | Bought each item |
| 3 | Jill Johnston | 2 | 1 | 2 | |
| 4 | Peter Jack | 0 | 1 | 2 | |
| 5 | Bart Simpson | 1 | 1 | 4 | |
| 6 | Ann Black | 1 | 0 | 1 | |
| 7 | | | | | |
| 8 | | | | | |

You could enter the data into a spreadsheet and use **AND** to return a TRUE value if a customer buys >0 of each item, and FALSE if they don't. In this example, you would create the function in E3 like this.

1 Click the **Insert Function** button.
2 Select AND from the function list (in the **Logical** category).
3 In the **Logical1** field, insert B3>0.
4 In the **Logical2** field, insert C3>0.
5 In the **Logical3** field, insert D3>0.
6 Click **OK**.

When you copy (AutoFill) the function down the column, you will get a TRUE message where ALL the conditions are met and a FALSE message where they are not.

## OR

The OR function will return a TRUE value if *any* condition in the function is met, and FALSE if none are met.

You could add another column to the example to identify customers who have bought more than 2 of any item that you sell.

1 Click the **Insert Function** button.
2 Select OR from the function list (in the **Logical** category).
3 In the **Logical1** field, insert B3>2 to check if the value in B3 is greater than 2.

**4** In the **Logical2** field, insert C3>2.

**5** In the **Logical2** field, insert D3>2.

**6** Click **OK**.

When you copy the function down the column, you will get a TRUE message where *any* condition is met and a FALSE message where none is.

You can combine IFs and ANDs and ORs in a variety of ways.

You could use a combination of IF and AND to identify those customers who had bought at least one of each item, and display a message saying that they qualify for a free Teddy Bear. Your **Function Arguments** would look something like the next screenshot – with the AND function *nested* within an IF.

**Function Arguments** — IF

| Logical_test | AND(B3>0,C3>0,D3>0) | = TRUE |
| Value_if_true | "Free Teddy Bear" | = "Free Teddy Bear" |
| Value_if_false | No Prize | = |

= "Free Teddy Bear"

Checks whether a condition is met, and returns one value if TRUE, and another value if FALSE.

**Value_if_false** is the value that is returned if Logical_test is FALSE. If omitted, FALSE is returned.

Formula result =     Free Teddy Bear

Help on this function      OK      Cancel

# 6.2 Statistical and Math functions

## COUNTIF and SUMIF

COUNTIF looks at a list of values and calculates how many of them satisfy specified criteria. It can be used when you're checking for **one** criterion. The syntax is =COUNTIF(Range,Criteria).

**1** Click the **Insert Function** button.

**2** Select **COUNTIF** from the list of functions.

**Function Arguments** — COUNTIF

| Range | D4:D28 | = {45;82;62;88;65;55... |
| Criteria | >=80 | = |

=

Counts the number of cells within a range that meet the given condition.

**Criteria** is the condition in the form of a number, expression, or text that defines which cells will be counted.

Formula result =

Help on this function      OK      Cancel

**3** Enter the range of cells that you want to be counted in the **Range** field.

**4** Specify the criteria that must be met for an entry to be counted in the **Criteria** field.

**5** Click **OK**.

The function could be used to count the number of students that obtained specific results in their exams.

The SUMIF function works in a similar way to the COUNTIF, but adds the values together if the condition is met.

# 6.3 Text functions

There are a number of Text functions that you may find useful from time to time. They are very easy to use. You could type up a list of names and experiment using the functions discussed.

## CONCATENATE

The **Concatenate** function displays the full name in column C.

**1** Click the **Insert Function** button.

**2** Select the **Concatenate** function.

**3** Enter the cell address for the first piece of text in **Text1**.

**4** Put a space – it could be any character – in **Text2** (in quotation marks). If you omit it, the words will run together.

**5** Enter the address of the cell that contains the next piece of text in **Text2**.

**6** Enter more text strings as required – you can have up to 30.

**7** Click **OK**.

## UPPER

**Upper** is a case change function. You can use it to change all the letters in a text entry to upper case. You could use **Upper** to display the full name in upper case in Column D.

1 Click the **Insert Function** button.

2 Select the **Upper** function.

3 Enter the cell address that contains the text you want to convert e.g. **C2**.

4 Click **OK**.

## LOWER

**Lower** changes all the letters in a text entry to lower case. You could use it to display the full name in lower case in Column E.

1 Click the **Insert Function** button.

2 Select the **Lower** function.

3 Enter the cell address that contains the text, e.g. **C2**.

4 Click **OK**.

## PROPER

**Proper** converts a text entry to initial capitals. You could use it to display the name with initial capitals in Column F.

1 Click the **Insert Function** button.

2 Select the **Proper** function.

3 Enter the cell address that contains the text, e.g. **C2**.

4 Click **OK**.

| | A | B | C | D | E | F |
|---|---|---|---|---|---|---|
| 1 | Firstname | Surname | Full Name | Full Name in UPPER case | Full Name in LOWER case | Full Name with Initial Caps |
| 2 | Gill | McLaren | =CONCATENATE(A2," ",B2) | =UPPER(C2) | =LOWER(C2) | =PROPER(C2) |
| 3 | Peter | Shaw | =CONCATENATE(A3," ",B3) | =UPPER(C3) | =LOWER(C3) | =PROPER(C3) |
| 4 | Kim | Stephen | =CONCATENATE(A4," ",B4) | =UPPER(C4) | =LOWER(C4) | =PROPER(C4) |
| 5 | Andrew | Borthwick | =CONCATENATE(A5," ",B5) | =UPPER(C5) | =LOWER(C5) | =PROPER(C5) |
| 6 | Alison | Peterson | =CONCATENATE(A6," ",B6) | =UPPER(C6) | =LOWER(C6) | =PROPER(C6) |
| 7 | Amanda | Mitchell | =CONCATENATE(A7," ",B7) | =UPPER(C7) | =LOWER(C7) | =PROPER(C7) |
| 8 | Gordon | Williamson | =CONCATENATE(A8," ",B8) | =UPPER(C8) | =LOWER(C8) | =PROPER(C8) |
| 9 | Clare | Stephen | =CONCATENATE(A9," ",B9) | =UPPER(C9) | =LOWER(C9) | =PROPER(C9) |
| 10 | Jack | Williamson | =CONCATENATE(A10," ",B10) | =UPPER(C10) | =LOWER(C10) | =PROPER(C10) |
| 11 | Ann | Shaw | =CONCATENATE(A11," ",B11) | =UPPER(C11) | =LOWER(C11) | =PROPER(C11) |
| 12 | Alison | Anderson | =CONCATENATE(A12," ",B12) | =UPPER(C12) | =LOWER(C12) | =PROPER(C12) |

# 6.4 Date functions

Date functions allow you to insert the current date and/or time into a cell on your worksheet (or into calculations), and display the date and/or time in a variety of ways.

## TODAY()

The TODAY() function enters the date from your computer clock into your worksheet. It's such a regularly used function that most people enter it directly through the keyboard.

**To insert the current day:**

**1** Select a cell in your worksheet.

**2** Type in **=TODAY()** – you *must* type in the = and the () to get the function to work.

**3** Press [**Enter**].

## NOW()

The NOW() function enters the date and time from your computer clock. Again, it is usually typed in through the keyboard.

**To insert the current day:**

**1** Select a cell in your worksheet.

**2** Type in **=NOW()** – you *must* type in the = and the ().

**3** Press [**Enter**].

* If the date and/or time are not correct when you use these functions you will need to reset the clock on your computer.

The values in the cells with the TODAY() or NOW() functions in them are *volatile*. They will be updated automatically each day as the date and time changes.

## DAY, MONTH and YEAR

The **DAY, MONTH** and **YEAR** functions can be used to display just the section of the date required. You can use the function to return the portion required from a date entered into a cell in your worksheet, or you can nest the TODAY or NOW function within it.

**To return part of a date already in a cell:**

**1** Select the cell that you want the DAY, MONTH or YEAR displayed in.

**2** Click the **Insert Function** button.

**3** Choose DAY, MONTH or YEAR from the function list.

| Function Arguments | | | | X |
|---|---|---|---|---|
| DAY | | | | |
| Serial_number | A1 | | ▦ = 37930 | |
| | | | = 5 | |
| Returns the day of the month, a number from 1 to 31. | | | | |
| Serial_number is a number in the date-time code used by Microsoft Office Excel. | | | | |
| Formula result = | 5 | | | |
| Help on this function | | | OK | Cancel |

**4** Enter the cell address in the **Serial_Number** field.

**5** Click **OK**.

**To enter part of the date from TODAY() or NOW():**

**1** Select the cell that you want the DAY, MONTH or YEAR in.

**2** Click the **Insert Function** button.

**3** Choose DAY, MONTH or YEAR from the function list.

| | Microsoft Excel - TY Exercises | | | | | | | _ □ X |
|---|---|---|---|---|---|---|---|---|
| | File Edit View Insert Format Tools Data Window Help | | | | | calculate dates | | _ ∂ X |
| Arial | ▾ 10 ▾ | B I U | ▐ ▐ ▐ ▐ | ▩ % , | ‰ ‱ | ⮑ ⮑ | □ ▾ ♦ ▾ A ▾ | |
| | H22 ▾ | | | | | | | |
| | A | B | C | D | E | F | G | H |
| 10 | Employee Name | Start Date | Length of Service (years) | | | | | |
| 11 | William Smith | 10/03/1965 | 38 | | | | | |
| 12 | Joyce Andrews | 01/07/2001 | 2 | | | | | |
| 13 | | | | | | | | |
| 14 | Student Name | Date of Birth | Age (years) | | | | | |
| 15 | Gill Adams | 10/11/1985 | 18 | | | | | |
| 16 | Peter Smith | 20/03/1981 | 22 | | | | | |
| 17 | | | | | | | | |
| 18 | Item | Delivery Date | Time in Stock (days) | | | | | |
| 19 | Chest of Drawers | 26/09/2003 | 40 | | | | | |
| 20 | Table | 01/07/2003 | 127 | | | | | |

Text Functions \ **Date & Time** / Customer

Ready                                                                        NUM

**4** Type 'TODAY()' or 'NOW()' in the **Serial_Number** field.

**5** Click **OK**.

The TODAY() and NOW() functions are useful when calculating things like age, length of service, or the length of time an item has been in stock.

## 6.5 Financial functions

Out of the many financial functions in Excel, those dealing with loans and investments are perhaps the ones that are most useful to us all, at a personal if not professional level. Three deal with the repayment of loans (which we all have to handle at some time!), and two are useful when working with savings and investments. The arguments used in these functions are:

| | |
|---|---|
| **pv** | the present (original) value of the loan |
| **pmt** | the repayment per period |
| **rate** | the interest rate per period |
| **nper** | the total number of payments |

The three functions that can be used with loans are:

**=PMT (rate, nper, pv)**

calculates the payment each period if the **pv**, **rate** and **nper** are known

=RATE (nper, pmt, pv)

calculates the interest rate when the **pmt**, **nper** and **pv** are known

=PV (rate, nper, pmt)

calculates the loan value when **rate**, **pmt** and **nper** are known

Functions that are useful when dealing with investments are:

=FV (rate, nper, pmt)

calculates the final value of saving an amount (**pmt**) for a specific time (**nper**) at a given interest **rate**

=NPV (rate, value1, value2...)

calculates the net present value of an investment using a comparison discount rate (**rate**) and a series of future income payments from the investment (positive values) and payments to the investment (negative payments). You can have up to 29 value arguments.

Have a look at (and experiment with) these examples of how these functions can be used. You'll find other examples (and more information on these functions) in the Help system.

## =PMT(rate, nper, pv)

You have decided to extend your house. Your architect estimates that it will cost £20,000. Your bank is prepared to give you a loan for this, at 10% interest per year, over 10 years. What is the monthly repayment on this loan?

You are working out a repayment, so you would use the **=PMT** function. The arguments would be:

=PMT(10%/12, 10*12, 20000)

10%/12 is the monthly interest repayment

10*12 is the number of repayments you will make

20000 is the amount you will borrow

*Your monthly repayments would be £264.30.*

## =RATE (nper, pmt, pv)

What is the interest rate of a 4-year loan for £10,000 with a monthly payment (at the end of the month) of £390?

=RATE (4*12,-390, 10000)

4*12 is the number of repayments

-390 is the amount that you repay each month

10000 is the amount of the loan

*The interest rate is 3%.*

## =PV (rate, nper, pmt)

You need to borrow some money to buy a car. You have calculated that the most you can afford to pay back each month is £250. Your bank is willing to offer you a loan, over 4 years, at 5% interest. How much can you afford to borrow?

=PV(5%/12,4*12,-250)

5%/12 is the interest rate per month

4*12 is the number of payments over the 4 years

-250 is the amount that you pay each month

*The amount you can afford to borrow is £10,855.74.*

## =FV (rate, nper, pmt)

You inherit £10,000 that is deposited in a savings account that pays 7% annual interest. If you deposit a further £1,000 at the end of each subsequent year, what will the savings account be worth in 10 years' time?

=FV(7%,10,-1000,-10000)

7% is the interest paid each year

10 is the number of payments

-1000 is the amount that you pay each year

-10000 is the amount when you opened the account (the pv)

*Your savings account will be worth £33,487.96.*

## =NPV (rate, value1, value2...)

You have just received a windfall payment of £20,000. You have decided to invest the money into a venture which will pay you an annual income of £7,200, £8,400 and £10,400 in the next three years. The current rate of interest is 7.5%. What is the NPV of your investment?

=NPV(7.5%,-20000,7200,8400,10400)

7.5% is the interest rate

-20000 is the initial payment (negative value as you paid it)

7200, 8400, 10400 are the amounts that you receive in the next three years (positive values as it is money you receive)

*The NPV of your investment would be £2,174.94.*

## 6.6 Lookup functions

You can locate values in a table array using the HLOOKUP (horizontal) or VLOOKUP (vertical) functions.

Use HLOOKUP when your comparison values are located in a row across the top of a table of data, and you want to look along a row to that column.

The format of the function is:

**=HOOKUP(Lookup value, table array, row number)**

You can identify the column using cell addresses or column labels.

Use VLOOKUP when your comparison values are located in a column to the left of the data you want to find, and you want to look down a column until the data is located.

**=VLOOKUP(Lookup value, table array, column number)**

You can identify the row using cell addresses or row labels.

**Microsoft Excel - TY Exercises**

File   Edit   View   Insert   Format   Tools   Data   Window   Help   Type a question for help

Arial    10    **B** *I* U

E14

| | A | B | C | D | E | F | G | H |
|---|---|---|---|---|---|---|---|---|
| 1 | Country | Life expectancy | Population (millions) | | HLOOKUP | | | |
| 2 | France | 76 | 56 | | 10.3 | Population of Portugal | | |
| 3 | Gambia | 44 | 0.8 | | 76 | Life expectancy in Italy | | |
| 4 | Germany | 75 | 77.6 | | | | | |
| 5 | Iceland | 78 | 0.3 | | | | | |
| 6 | Italy | 76 | 57.1 | | VLOOKUP | | | |
| 7 | Mozambique | 47 | 15.2 | | 44 | Life expectancy in Gambia | | |
| 8 | Portugal | 74 | 10.3 | | 39.1 | Population of Spain | | |
| 9 | Spain | 77 | 39.1 | | | | | |
| 10 | UK | 76 | 57.1 | | | | | |
| 11 | | | | | | | | |
| 12 | | | | | | | | |

Date & Time   Customer Purchase Data

Ready                                                                 NUM

# 6.7 Data tables

A data table is a range of values that can be substituted into a formula. There are two types of data tables – one-variable (where one value in the formula is substituted) and two-variable (where two values are substituted).

## One-variable data table

In a one-variable data table, the values can be listed down a column or across a row. In this example, we have a distance of 4000 miles to travel, and want to work out how long it will take. We can use a one-variable data table to show this – the time depends on the speed at which we travel (the variable). The basic formula to calculate the time taken will be Distance/Speed.

1   Enter the distance that you need to travel in a cell, e.g. **B2**.

2   Enter the variable data (the speeds that you could average each hour) either across one row or down one column, e.g. **A5:A8**.

To create a column-orientated table:

1   Type the formula (**B2/E2**) that refers to the input cell in the row above the first value and one cell to the right of the column of values, e.g. **B4**. Type any additional formulas to the right of the first formula.

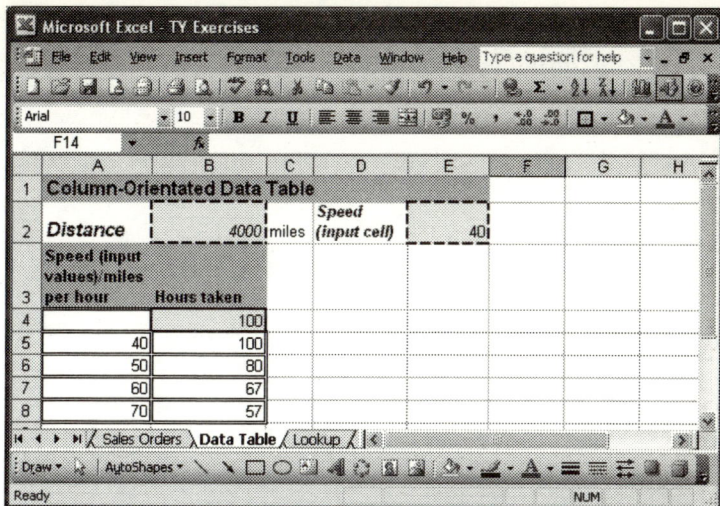

**2** Select the range of cells that contain the formulas *and* values that you want to substitute – **A4:B8**.

**3** On the **Data** menu, click **Table**.

**4** Type the cell reference for the input cell in the **Column input cell** box – ours is **E2**.

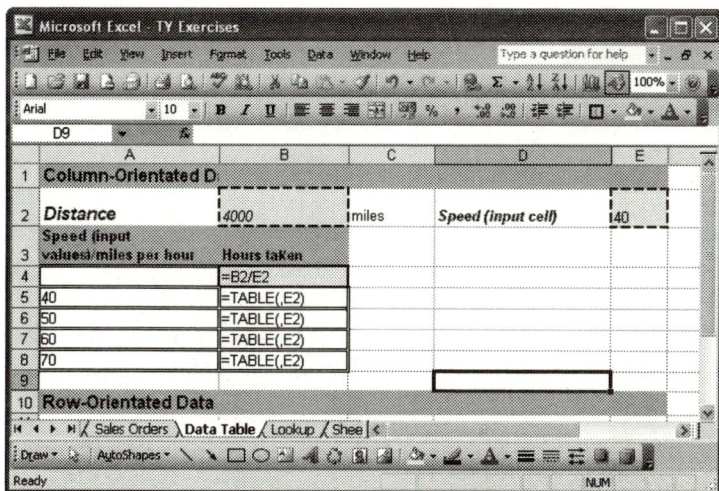

## To create a row-oriented table:

1 Type the formula in the column to the left of the first value and one cell below the row of values. Type any additional formulas below the first formula.

2 Select the range of cells that contain the formulas and values you want to substitute.

3 On the **Data** menu, click **Table**.

4 Type the reference for the input cell in the **Row input cell** box.

## Two-variable data table

A two-variable input table is very similar, but with a row and a column input value. You could create a two-variable input table to calculate the 'times tables' from 1 to 12.

1 Enter the formula that refers to the two input cells in a cell on the worksheet (in **B4** in this example).

2 Enter one list of input values in the same column, below the formula.

3 Enter the second list of input values in the same row, to the right of the formula.

**4** Select the range of cells that contains the formula and both the row and column of values (**B4:N16**).

**5** Open the **Data** menu, and choose **Table**.

**6** In the **Row input cell** box, enter the reference to the input cell for the input values in the row.

**7** In the **Column input cell** box, enter the reference to the input cell for the input values in the column.

**8** Click **OK**.

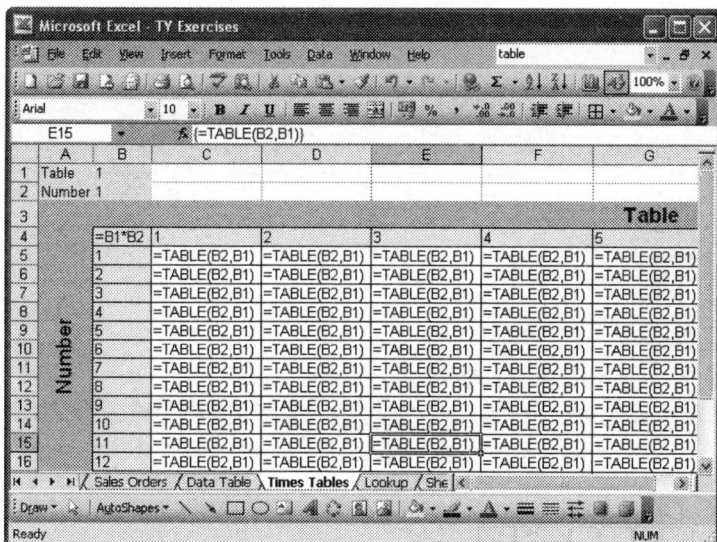

- Go to one-variable and two-variable data tables in Help for more information.

# 6.8 Scenarios

A scenario is a named set of values that can be applied to a set of selected cells in your workbook. They are used when you want to set up a model where you can quickly substitute the inputs so that you can compare the solutions. They are useful in 'What If' situations, where you can set up several named inputs and apply them to your worksheet to help identify best and worst cases.

Let's say you wanted to perform some calculations to work out the monthly repayments that you would have to make on a loan. You are considering three options.

| | Amount of loan | Interest rate | Payback period |
|---|---|---|---|
| Option 1 | £20,000 | 7% | 5 years |
| Option 2 | £25,000 | 7% | 8 years |
| Option 3 | £30,000 | 10% | 12 years |

You could set up each option as a scenario.

**1** Set up your worksheet to show the Option 1 payments and input the formula required.

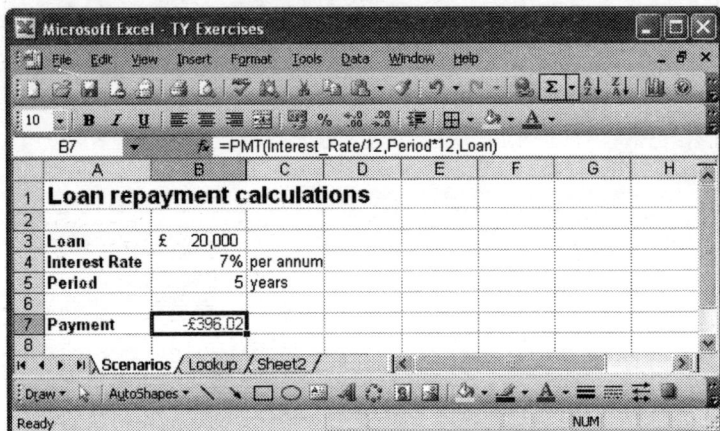

**2** Open the **Tools** menu.

**3** Select **Scenarios...**

**4** At the **Scenario Manager** dialog box click **Add...**

**5** Give the scenario a name, e.g. **Option 1**.

**6** Specify the cells that will change when you show the various scenarios, e.g. **B3:B5** and click **OK**.

**7** Type the values in for Option 1 and click **Add**.

**8** Repeat steps **5–7** for Option 2 and 3.

**9** Click **OK**.

The scenarios will be listed in the Scenario Manager dialog box. If a scenario is wrong or no longer required, you can edit or delete it from here.

To see the repayment options, select one and click **Show** – the values on your sheet will be substituted by those in the scenario. When you show each in turn, you can see the outcome of that scenario only. If you wish to see the outcomes of all the scenarios at once (to compare them) you must create a scenario summary.

**1** Display the **Scenario Manager** dialog box.

**2** Click **Summary...**

**3** Choose **Scenario summary** as the report type and edit the **Result cells** field if necessary.

**4** Click **OK**.

A new worksheet will be created showing the summary report.

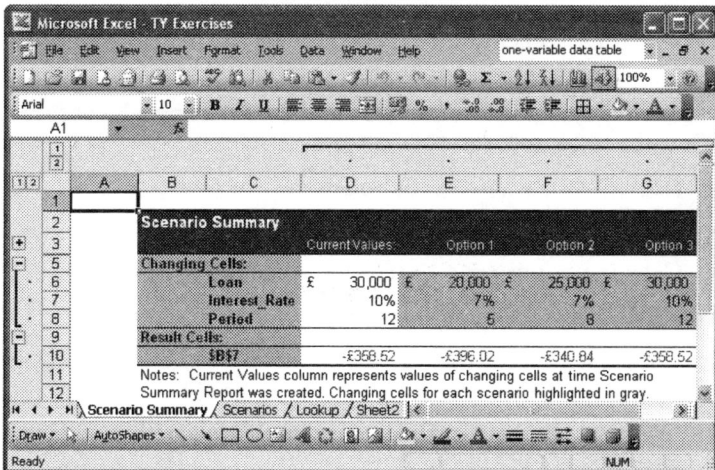

# 6.9 PivotTable

There may be times when you want to create a report that summarizes the data held in a worksheet. You might want to perform some calculations on the summarized data, or filter it to display specific data from the list. PivotTables can be used in this situation. They are interactive tables that allow you to summarize large amounts of data.

A PivotTable consists of four areas – page, column, row and data.

The page, column and row areas show the data that you have added to the PivotTable – they act as labels for the data that you are summarizing. They are also used to filter the data that you add.

The data area is where the summary result calculations are performed and displayed. Each item in the data area must have a function associated with it – sum, average, count, etc.

| Page | | Column |
|------|------|--------|
| | Row | Data |

You don't **have** to have an item in the page, column or row area, but you **must** have something in the data area (you have to be summarizing something!).

In this example we've used Excel to record details of customer orders. We then go on to summarize this data using a PivotTable. We want to be able to:

• Display the order data by town.

• Filter the data to show the order data from each customer.

♦ Calculate totals for the number of each item purchased.

**To create a PivotTable to do this:**

**1** Click anywhere inside the list of data for which you want to create a PivotTable.

**2** Open the **Data** menu and choose **PivotTable and Pivot Chart Report...**

Microsoft Excel - TY Exercises

| | A | B | C | D | E | F | G | H |
|---|---|---|---|---|---|---|---|---|
| 1 | | | **Gerry's Garden Centre** | | | | | |
| 2 | | | | | | | | |
| 3 | Order Summary for | | December | | | | | |
| 4 | | | | | | | | |
| 5 | Order ID | Date | Customer | Town | Roses | Lilies | Carnations | |
| 6 | FF100 | 01/12/2003 | Fabby Flowers | Edinburgh | 30 | 10 | 20 | |
| 7 | GT001 | 03/12/2003 | Golden Tulip | Dalkeith | 20 | 20 | 40 | |
| 8 | AF001 | 03/12/2003 | Amy's Flowers | Edinburgh | 50 | 60 | 80 | |
| 9 | FF101 | 04/12/2003 | Fabby Flowers | Edinburgh | 22 | 10 | 50 | |
| 10 | AF002 | 04/12/2003 | Amy's Flowers | Edinburgh | 60 | 30 | 20 | |
| 11 | GT002 | 06/12/2003 | Golden Tulip | Dalkeith | 16 | 22 | 30 | |
| 12 | BB001 | 06/12/2003 | Best Blooms | Dalkeith | 10 | 20 | 30 | |
| 13 | GT003 | 07/12/2003 | Golden Tulip | Dalkeith | 20 | 18 | 30 | |
| 14 | AF003 | 07/12/2003 | Amy's Flowers | Edinburgh | 60 | 50 | 90 | |
| 15 | FF102 | 08/12/2003 | Fabby Flowers | Edinburgh | 16 | 20 | 30 | |
| 16 | GT004 | 08/12/2002 | Golden Tulip | Dalkeith | 20 | 24 | 30 | |
| 17 | FF103 | 10/12/2003 | Fabby Flowers | Edinburgh | 18 | 22 | 50 | |
| 18 | BB002 | 10/12/2003 | Best Blooms | Dalkeith | 20 | 20 | 20 | |
| 19 | GT005 | 11/12/2003 | Golden Tulip | Dalkeith | 14 | 20 | 70 | |
| 20 | GT006 | 12/12/2002 | Golden Tulip | Dalkeith | 14 | 16 | 60 | |
| 21 | FF104 | 15/12/2003 | Fabby Flowers | Edinburgh | 16 | 20 | 80 | |
| 22 | BB003 | 15/12/2003 | Best Blooms | Dalkeith | 30 | 50 | 70 | |
| 23 | GT006 | 16/12/2003 | Golden Tulip | Dalkeith | 20 | 30 | 50 | |

3 Select **Microsoft Excel List or database** and **PivotTable** at step 1 of the wizard and click **Next**.

4 Check the range (and edit if necessary) at step 2 of the wizard, then click **Next**.

5 At step 3, choose the location for the PivotTable – if you want it in the existing worksheet, enter the cell address for the top left corner of the PivotTable.

PivotTable and PivotChart Wizard - Step 3 of 3

Where do you want to put the PivotTable report?

⊙ New worksheet
○ Existing worksheet

Click Finish to create your PivotTable report.

[ Layout... ] [ Options... ] [ Cancel ] [ < Back ] [ Next > ] [ Finish ]

**6** Click **Finish**.

An empty PivotTable will be displayed, with the Field list and PivotTable toolbar displayed. You can now lay out your PivotTable onscreen.

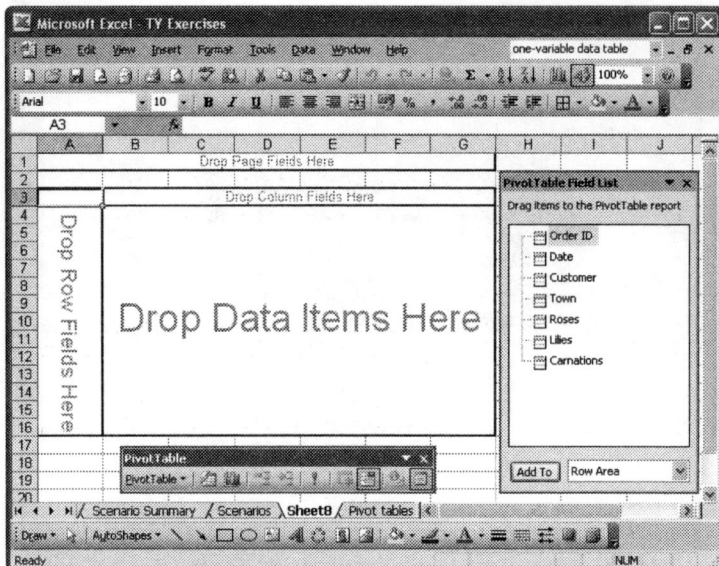

Drag the items from the field list and drop them in the area that you want them to be in on the PivotTable. Any fields that you want to be able to filter your data by should be in the Page, Column or Row fields. Data that will be summarized goes in the Data area.

**Drag the:**

- **Town** field to the **Page** area.
- **Customer** to the **Column** area.
- **Roses**, **Lilies** and **Carnations** to the **Data** area.
- Close the field list.
- You can **pivot** the data in your PivotTable by dragging the fields from one area to another – watch the mouse pointer as you do this – it gives you a clue as to what area you are over!
- **Filter** your data using the drop-down arrows at the Page, Row and Column area.

This section has given an introduction to PivotTables – experiment with them and visit the Help system for more information.

## Summary

In this chapter we have discussed:

* Logical functions – IF, AND, OR

* Statistical and math functions – COUNTIF and SUMIF

* Text functions – concatenate, upper, lower, proper

* Date functions – today, now, day, month, and year

* Financial functions that are used when dealing with loans and investments

* Lookup functions

* Data tables

* Scenarios

* PivotTables

# 07

# charting and drawing

## In this chapter you will learn:

- how to produce charts from your data
- about printing charts
- how to add special effects to your charts
- about the Drawing tools

## Aims of this chapter

Pictures often speak louder than words (and numbers). This chapter discusses Excel's excellent charting capabilities – they're easy to use and look great. We'll also look at how the drawing toolbar can be used to enhance charts and data.

# 7.1 Preparing your data

Excel can create charts – bar graphs, line graphs, pie charts, scatter diagrams, etc. – from the data in your worksheet.

You can create your chart on the same worksheet as the data on which the chart is built (an embedded chart), or on a separate chart sheet.

- *Ideally* the data should be in adjacent cells.

- If there are blank rows or columns within the data to be charted, remove these before you try to chart it.

**To chart data that is not in adjacent cells:**

**1** Select the first group of cells you want to chart.

**2** Hold down [**Ctrl**] while you click and drag over the other groups you want to include in your chart.

- When the non-adjacent cells are selected, the areas *must* be able to combine to form a rectangle.

## 7.2 Chart Wizard

The Chart Wizard is used to step you through the process of setting up your chart.

**To chart the data in your worksheet:**

**1** Select the data you want to chart – including the column headings and row labels.

**2** Click the **Chart Wizard** tool 📊 on the Standard toolbar.

**3** At Step 1 of the Chart Wizard, select the **Chart type**.

There are over a dozen basic chart types and unlimited variations

**4** Click the **Press and Hold to View Sample** button to see what your data would look like in your chosen chart type.

**5** Once you've decided on a type, click **Next**.

**6** At Step 2, on the **Data Range** tab, check the data range selected, decide whether you want to display the data series in rows or columns (try both and decide which you prefer). Click **Next**.

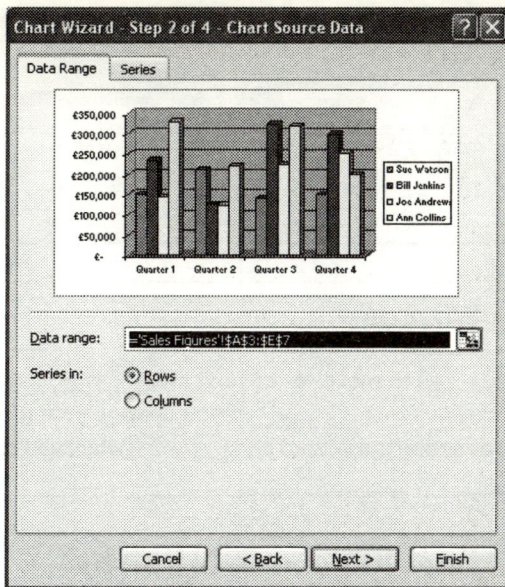

- Once a chart has been created, changes made to the data on which the chart is based, will automatically be reflected in the chart. This happens regardless of whether the chart is an object in your worksheet, or on a separate chart sheet.

**7** At Step 3, explore the various tabs in the **Chart Options** dialog box and select the options you require. Click **Next**.

**8** Decide where the chart should be located – in your worksheet, or on a separate chart sheet. Click **Finish**.

### Using Wizards

Click [ Next > ] to move to the next step, [ < Back ] to return to the previous one, [ Cancel ] if you change your mind and want to abandon the Wizard and [ Finish ] when you're done.

## 7.3 A chart in your worksheet

Once you've created a chart, the Chart toolbar will be displayed.

The chart will be selected – indicated by handles in each corner and along each side.

If you click on the worksheet area, the chart becomes deselected, and the Chart toolbar disappears.

To select the chart again, click on it once. The **Chart** menu appears in the menu bar when the chart is selected.

### Chart objects

Each area of a chart is an object – you have a chart area object, plot area object, category axis object, legend object, etc.

**To select a chart object:**

• Choose the object from the **Chart Objects** list `Chart Area`.

Or

• Click on the object you want to select.

## Move, resize and delete charts

If you want to move, resize or delete a chart that is an object on a worksheet, you must first select the chart area – either point to the chart area within the chart and click (a prompt will tell you what the mouse is pointing at) or choose **Chart Area** from the **Chart Objects** list on the **Chart** toolbar.

**To move the chart:**

1  Select the chart.

2  Point to the chart area using the mouse – a prompt will appear to tell you what area you are pointing at.

3  Drag the chart to its new position.

**To resize the chart:**

1  Select the chart.

2  Point to one of the handles along the edge of the chart area.

3  Drag the handle to increase or decrease the size of the object.

**To delete the chart:**

1  Select the chart.

2  Press [**Delete**] on your keyboard.

## Formatting chart objects

You can change the formatting of each object in your chart to get the effect you want.

**To format an object in your chart:**

1  Choose the object required from the **Chart Objects** list.

2  Click the **Format** tool on the Chart toolbar.

Or

• Double-click the chart object you want to format.

When the **Format** dialog box appears, explore it to see the formatting options you have. Experiment with the options until you find the right formatting for your chart. For example:

* To change the position of the legend, double-click on it, then use the **Placement** tab in the **Format** dialog box.

* To change the colour of the plot area, double-click on it, then select the colour required from the dialog box.

* To remove or edit the gridlines, double-click on them, then use the **Patterns** or **Scale** tabs to specify your requirements.

* If you want to format the font of an object, use the tools on the Formatting toolbar – font, size, bold, italic, etc.

## To change the chart type

If your chart doesn't look the way you expected, and you think a different chart type would be better, you can change the type at any time.

**To change the chart type:**

1 Click the drop-down arrow to the right of the **Chart Type** tool [icon] on the Chart toolbar.

2 Select the type of chart required.

## Other options

If you explore the menus when your chart is selected, you will find that some of the worksheet menu options have disappeared, and options specific to charting have appeared. The **Format** and **Chart** menus contain most of the charting options.

**In the Chart menu choose:**

* **Chart Type...** to return to the dialog box displayed at Step 1 of the Wizard. This gives you access to all the chart types and sub-types.

* **Source Data...** to return to Step 2 of the Wizard. If you need to edit the data range, this is the best place to do it.

* **Chart Options...** to return to the options at Step 3. You can add titles, change the position of the legend, edit the gridlines, etc. through this dialog box.

- ◆ **Location...** to return to the dialog box displayed at Step 4 of the Wizard. You can change the location of the selected chart from here – useful if you want to move it to another sheet, or decide to put it on a separate chart sheet.

# 7.4 A chart on a separate sheet

If you opt to locate your chart in a new sheet, your chart will be displayed on a sheet called *Chart1* (unless you've already got a Chart1 sheet, in which case it will be in the Chart2 sheet and so on). The chart sheet is inserted to the left of the worksheet from which it gets its data.

The Chart toolbar is displayed when the chart sheet is selected. You can use the Chart toolbar, or the **Format** or **Chart** menu to modify the chart as required.

You can rename the sheet, move it to another location in your workbook, or delete it if you decide you don't need it any more (see Chapter 4 for renaming, moving and deleting sheets).

# 7.5 Charts without the Wizard

Charts can be created very quickly, missing out the steps you work through with the Chart Wizard. The charts created use the default chart layout – this is a column chart (unless it has been changed on your machine – see section 7.7).

**To create an embedded chart:**

**1** Select the cells you want to chart.

**2** Click the **Default Chart** tool 🖼 – if the tool it not displayed, you can add it to a toolbar (see Chapter 11).

**3** Drag the chart into position on the sheet.

**To create a chart on a separate chart sheet:**

**1** Select the cells you want to chart.

**2** Press [**F11**].

The charts you create can be formatted and printed in the same way as those created using the Chart Wizard.

# 7.6 Printing your chart

You can print your chart with or without the data on which it is based. If it is an object in a worksheet you have several print options. Check it through Print Preview before you print.

**To print the chart and all of the data on the worksheet:**

• Print the worksheet as normal (with the chart deselected).

**To get a printout of the chart only:**

• Select the chart on the worksheet, then print.

**To print the chart, plus its data, but no other data:**

◆ Select the chart and click the **Data Table** tool ▦ on the Chart toolbar to display the data table for the chart. Print out with the chart selected.

**To print a chart that is on a separate chart sheet:**

**1** Select the chart sheet.

**2** Print as usual.

◆ If you also want to print out the data on which the chart is based, display the data table before you print.

If printing in black and white, go to Page Setup and select the option on the Chart tab

## 7.7 Default chart

The default chart in Excel is a column chart. If you don't use
column charts very often, you can change the default chart type.

**To change the default chart type:**

1  Open the **Chart** menu and choose **Chart Type...**
2  Select the chart type and subtype you want as your default.
3  Click the **Set as default chart** button.
4  Click **Yes** to change the default type, **No** to cancel the change.

Microsoft Excel

Are you sure that you want to use a Bar chart type as the default for creating new charts?

- To use this chart type as the default for all future charts, click Yes. The program will automatically use this chart type when creating a chart, but you can change the chart type after it's created.
- To cancel changing the default chart type, click No.

Yes    No

## 7.8 Special effects

One of the best ways to find out about the charting capabilities
is to experiment. However, here are some tips and pointers if
you want to get that little bit more from your charts!

Format Axis

Patterns    Scale    Font    Number    Alignment

Value (Z) axis scale

Auto

☐ Minimum:        10000
☑ Maximum:        350000
☑ Major unit:     50000
☑ Minor unit:     10000
☑ Floor (XY plane)
   Crosses at:     0

Display units:    Thousands ▼    ☑ Show display units label on chart

☐ Logarithmic scale
☐ Values in reverse order
☐ Floor (XY plane) crosses at minimum value

OK    Cancel

## Value (Y-axis) scale

By default, the value axis starts at 0. If you don't have any small
values to plot, e.g. if all your values are 100,000 and over, this
results in a large 'dead' area at the bottom of your chart. You
can get rid of this area if you set an appropriate minimum value
for the axis.

1 Double-click the value axis.

2 Amend the values on the **Scale** tab as required.

3 Click **OK**.

• You can also amend the Display units setting from this tab.

## Overlaps and gap widths

The spacing between each bar or column on a chart is called the
'overlap'. The space between each group of bars or columns is
the 'gap width'. You can adjust these settings from the **Format
Data Series** dialog box.

1 Double-click any data series to open the **Format Data
Series** dialog box.

2 Select the **Options** tab.

3 Set the **Overlap** and/or **Gap** settings as required.

4 Click **OK**.

## Picture series

If you explore the **Patterns** tab in the **Format Data Series** dialog box you will find lots of colours and effects that you can use for each data series if you wish.

If you want a very special effect however, you could consider putting a *picture* into a data series – perhaps a £ or € symbol, or a pile of currency!

**To display a picture in the data series:**

1 Insert a picture from clip art or Microsoft Gallery into your worksheet (check out the online Help if necessary).

2 Copy the picture (select it and click the **Copy** tool).

3 Select the series that you want the picture displayed in.

4 Click **Paste**.

## Combined charts

You can customize your charts further by combining some chart types (you can't combine all types – experiment with them).

**To combine a column chart with a line chart:**

1 Display a column chart in 2-D (**Chart Type** tool).

2 Select the series that you wish to display as a line.

3 Choose **Line Chart** from the **Chart Type** list.

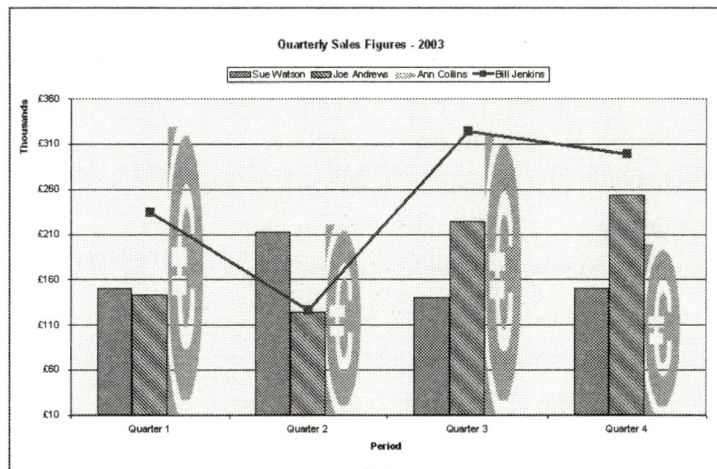

# 7.9 Drawing tools

You can use the Drawing toolbar to add different effects to your charts and data, e.g. you could draw an arrow, with a message attached, pointing to an object within your chart.

To display the Drawing toolbar:

♦ Click the Drawing tool 🔲 on the Standard toolbar.

## Line, Arrow, Rectangle and Oval

The basic tools are the Line, Arrow, Rectangle and Oval. You can use these tools to draw basic lines and shapes.

**1** Click the tool 🔲 .

**2** Click and drag to draw the shape.

For a perfect square or circle, select the Rectangle or Oval tool, and hold down [Shift] as you click and drag.

To do any work on an object, you must select it first. Deselect when you have done.

To resize or move your drawing objects:

**1** Click and drag a 'handle' to resize the object.

**2** Click and drag within the object to move it.

To add a shadow or 3-D effect to your object:

**1** Click the Shadow tool 🔲 or 3-D tool 🔲 .

**2** Choose the effect you want.

To change a line or arrow style of an object:

**1** Click the Line 🔲, Dash 🔲 or Arrow Style tool 🔲 .

**2** Choose the effect you want from the drop-down list.

**To change the fill colour, line colour or font colour of an object:**

**1** Click the drop-down arrow to the right of the **Fill** 🔲 or **Line Color** tool 🔲 or the **Font Color** tool 🔲.

**2** Choose a colour.

**To delete a drawing object:**

♦ Press [**Delete**].

## Text boxes

You can add text anywhere if it is contained within a text box.

**To insert a text box:**

**1** Click the **Text box** tool 🔲.

**2** Click and drag within the document to create the text box.

**3** Type in the text and format it if required.

**4** Click outside the text box to end.

## AutoShapes

If you want to draw stars, banners, block arrows, flow chart symbols, etc. you may find the shape you need in the AutoShapes. These are just as easy to use as the basic shapes above.

**1** Click the **AutoShapes** tool `AutoShapes ▾`.

**2** Choose a category.

**3** Select a shape.

**4** Click and drag to draw your shape.

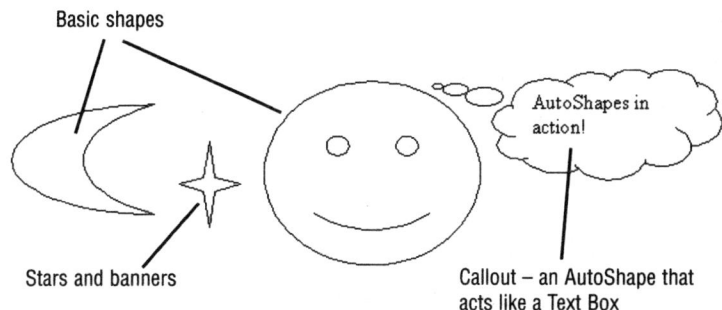

Basic shapes

AutoShapes in action!

Stars and banners

Callout – an AutoShape that acts like a Text Box

# 7.10 Some more options

**Draw** on the Drawing toolbar gives access to more options.

## Grouping

If you are drawing a picture using different drawing objects, you will find that your final picture is easier to resize and move if you *Group* the objects together.

Before you can group several objects, you must select them.

**To select more than one object at a time:**

1 Select the first object required – click on it.

2 Hold down [**Shift**] while you click on each of the other objects.

Or

1 Click the **Select Objects** tool ▒ on the Drawing toolbar.

2 Click and drag over the objects you want to select.

**To group objects:**

1 Select the objects you want to group.

2 Click the drop-down arrow to the right of **Draw** on the Drawing toolbar.

3 Choose **Group**.

The objects are grouped together into one object and can then be resized, moved or deleted as one. If you need to work on an individual object that has been grouped, you can ungroup the object again.

**To ungroup an object:**

1 Select the object you want to ungroup.

2 Click the drop-down arrow to the right of **Draw**.

3 Choose **Ungroup**.

4 Deselect the objects.

**To regroup objects that have been ungrouped:**

1 Click the drop-down arrow to the right of **Draw**.

2 Choose **Regroup**.

## Bring Forward, Send Backward

When you draw your objects on top of each other, the first one you draw is on the lowest layer, the second one is on a layer above the first one, the third one on the next layer and so on.

If your objects are on the wrong layer relative to each other, you can move them backwards and forwards through the layers as necessary.

**To move an object from one layer to another:**

1 Select the object.

2 Choose **Order** from the **Draw** options.

3 Move the object backwards or forwards as required.

| | |
|---|---|
| | Bring to Front |
| | Send to Back |
| | Bring Forward |
| | Send Backward |

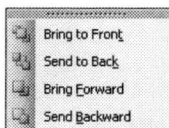

• **Bring to Front** and **Send to Back** move the object to the top or bottom layer respectively.

• **Bring Forward** and **Send Backward** move the object one layer at a time.

## Rotate and Flip

Objects can be rotated left or right 90°, or freely through any angle, or flipped horizontally or vertically.

Rotate handle

**To rotate an object:**

1 Select the object.

2 Click and drag the rotate handle (small green circle) until the object is in the position required.

**To flip an object:**

1 Select the object.

2 Choose **Rotate or Flip** from the Draw menu.

3 Select a rotate or flip option.

You can use the drawing tools to create different effects on your worksheet data and charts. If you create charts, try using an Arrow and a Text Box to add emphasis to it!

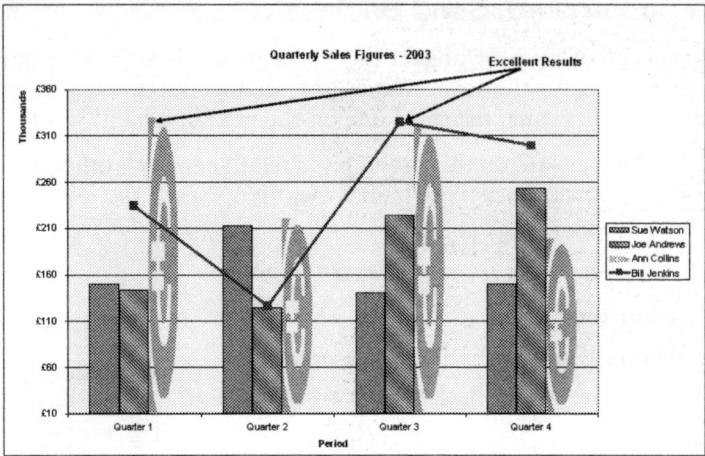

Quarterly Sales Figures - 2003

---

## Summary

In this chapter we have discussed:

- Preparing data for charting
- The Chart Wizard
- Charts embedded in worksheets
- Charts on separate sheets
- Producing charts without using the Chart Wizard
- Printing charts
- Changing the default chart
- Special effects on charts
- The Drawing toolbar
- Manipulating drawn objects

# 08

# autoformat, styles and templates

**In this chapter you will learn:**

- how to format your data using AutoFormat
- how to use, create and edit Styles
- about workbook and worksheet templates

## Aims of this chapter

In this chapter we will discuss some of the ways you can automate the formatting and page layout of your worksheet. We considered several formatting and page layout options in Chapter 3. In this chapter we will discuss how AutoFormat, Styles and Templates can make you more efficient when formatting.

# 8.1 AutoFormat

Instead of formatting your worksheet manually (as discussed in Chapter 3), you could try the AutoFormats. The AutoFormats are layouts that are already set up in Excel, and they can be applied to any area of your worksheet.

If you don't select an area of your worksheet before applying an AutoFormat, Excel will apply the AutoFormat to everything surrounding the current cell, until it reaches an empty row and/or column.

If you want to apply the AutoFormat to an area that includes empty rows and/or columns, make sure you select the whole area first.

**To apply an AutoFormat:**

1  Select the area (if necessary).

2  Open the **Format** menu and choose **AutoFormat...**

3  Scroll through the list and choose a format.

4  Click the **Options** button and deselect any options you don't want to apply.

5  Click **OK**.

## 8.2 Introducing styles

A style is a set of formatting options that you save as a group. When you want to apply the formats held in a style, you apply the style rather than each formatting option individually.

If you don't apply a style to the text or data you enter into your worksheet, it is formatted using the Normal style.

If you format your data using the Currency, Comma Style or Percent style tools on the Formatting toolbar you are applying a style that has already been set up in Excel. Other predefined styles are: Currency (0 decimal places), Comma (0 decimal places), Followed Hyperlink and Hyperlink. These styles can be located in the Style dialog box (see section 8.3) or through the Style tool which can be added to the toolbar (see Chapter 11).

Using styles has two main benefits:

♦  Consistency – when you apply a style, all the formatting options contained within it are applied in one go (you won't accidentally use the wrong font size or colour).

♦  Speed – it's usually quicker to apply a style than to apply formatting options using the Format Cells dialog box.

## 8.3 Working with styles

You can apply existing styles to your cells, edit existing styles, create styles of your own and delete styles you no longer use.

**To apply an existing style:**

1  Select the range of cells you want to format.

2  Choose **Style...** from the **Format** menu.

**3** Select the style you want to use from the **Style name** list.

**4** Click **OK**.

• You can click the style tools on the Formatting toolbar to apply currency , comma  and  percent styles.

**To modify an existing style:**

**1** Choose **Style...** from the **Format** menu.

**2** Select the style to modify from the **Style name** list.

**3** Click the **Modify...** button.

**4** Make the changes required in the **Format Cells** dialog box.

**5** Click **OK** to return to the **Style** dialog box.

**6** Click **OK** to return to your worksheet.

**To create a new style:**

**1** Choose **Style...** from the **Format** menu.

**2** Enter a new name for the style in the **Style name** list.

**3** Work through steps 3–5 above to define the style.

**4** Click **Add** to add the style to the list *without* applying the style to the selected cell, then click **Close**.

Or

**5** Click **OK** to add the style to the list and apply it to the selected cell.

**To delete a style:**

**1** Choose **Style...** from the **Format** menu.

**2** Select the style you want to delete from the **Style name** list.

**3** Click the **Delete** button.

**4** Click **OK**.

- You cannot delete the Normal style.

- If you delete the Currency, Comma or Percent style, you will not be able to use their tools on the Formatting toolbar.

If you have styles already set up in one workbook, and decide you want to use them in another workbook, you can copy the styles over.

**To copy styles from one workbook to another:**

**1** Open the workbook that contains the styles you want to copy.

**2** Open the workbook that you want to copy the styles into.

**3** Choose **Style...** from the **Format** menu.

**4** Click the **Merge** button.

**5** Double-click the workbook that contains the styles you want to copy.

- If the destination workbook already contains styles of the same name, you will be asked to confirm whether or not you want the styles copied.

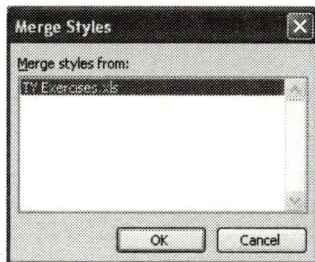

**6** Click **OK**.

- Styles can be applied and edited from the **Style** tool. If you intend to use styles, I suggest you add this tool to one of your toolbars (see section 11.4) – perhaps the Formatting one.

# 8.4 Workbook templates

A template is the pattern on which a workbook or worksheet is based. Up until now, your workbooks have been based on the default template. This is the one used to create a new workbook when you start Excel, or when you click the **New** tool, or choose **Workbook** from the **General** tab in the **Templates** dialog box.

If you intend to create different workbooks that follow the same basic layout, you could create a *custom* template for them. The template would contain the standard elements of the workbooks, e.g. standard text, column and row headings, formulas, headers and footers, styles, etc.

**To create a custom workbook template:**

1 Create a new workbook.

2 Insert or delete sheets as necessary to get the number of sheets you require in this template.

3 Add any standard text, formatting, formulas, headers/footers, styles, etc. to the workbook.

4 If you want a preview of your workbook to be displayed in the **New** dialog box, choose **Properties** from the **File** menu. On the **Summary** tab in the **Properties** dialog box, select the **Save preview picture** checkbox and click **OK**.

5 Click the **Save** tool on the Standard toolbar.

6 In the **Save as type** field, choose *Template*.

7 Select the *Templates* folder in the **Save in** field (if necessary).

8 Type in a name for the template in the **File name** field.

9 Click **Save**.

10 Close your template when you've finished.

**To create a new workbook using your custom template:**

1 Choose **New** from the **File** menu.

2 Click **On My Computer...** on the Task Pane.

**3** Select a template from the **General** tab in the **Templates** dialog box.

**4** Click **OK**.

## 8.5 Worksheet templates

You can also create templates for the worksheets you add to your workbooks.

**To create a custom worksheet template:**

**1** Create a new workbook consisting of *one* sheet only.

**2** Add any standard text, formatting, formulas, headers/footers, styles, etc. to the worksheet.

**3** If you want a preview of your worksheet to be displayed in the **Insert** dialog box, choose **Properties** from the **File** menu. On the **Summary** tab in the **Properties** dialog box, select the **Save preview picture** checkbox and click **OK**.

**4** Click the **Save** tool on the Standard toolbar.

**5** In the **Save as type** field, choose *Template*.

**6** Select the *Templates* folder in the **Save in** field (if necessary).

**7** Type in a name for the template in the **File name** field.

**8** Click **Save**.

**9** Close the worksheet template.

**To insert a custom worksheet template:**

1 Right-click on the sheet tab and click **Insert...** from the shortcut menu.

2 Select your worksheet template from the **General** tab in the **Insert** dialog box.

3 Click **OK**.

The new sheet will be inserted to the left of the selected one.

---

## Summary

In this chapter we have discussed:

- Autoformat
- Using standard Excel styles
- Editing styles
- Creating your own styles
- Designing a custom workbook template
- Creating a new workbook using your custom template
- Creating a custom worksheet template
- Inserting a custom worksheet template into a workbook

# 09

# list management

**In this chapter you will learn:**

- how to sort data
- about filtering data
- how to validate data
- how to insert subtotals
- how to manipulate data using Database functions

## Aims of this chapter

This chapter discusses how a list of data can be manipulated using basic database commands. It then looks at subtotals and some numeric database functions.

# 9.1 Terminology

Lists of stock items, customer names and phone numbers, exam results, etc. can all be manipulated using the list management features in Excel. You can sort, find and filter data in lists. The functions that you can perform on a list are similar to those you would expect to carry out on a database table in Microsoft Access. Because of the similarity between list manipulation and working with database tables, database terminology is used when working with lists of data in this way.

• Each row is a **record** in your list.

• Each column is a **field**.

• The column headings are the **field names**.

| | A | B | C | D | E | F | G | H |
|---|---|---|---|---|---|---|---|---|
| 1 | END OF TERM EXAM RESULTS | | | | | | | |
| 2 | | | | | | | | |
| 3 | Firstname | Surname | Computing % | Maths % | English % | Average Mark | Result | Grade |
| 4 | Gill | McLaren | 60 | 45 | 80 | 62 | Pass | B |
| 5 | Peter | Shaw | 77 | 82 | 80 | 80 | Pass | A |
| 6 | Kim | Stephen | 55 | 62 | 92 | 70 | Pass | B |
| 7 | Andrew | Borthwick | 50 | 88 | 74 | 71 | Pass | A |
| 8 | Alison | Peterson | 75 | 65 | 82 | 74 | Pass | A |
| 9 | Amanda | Mitchell | 63 | 55 | 72 | 63 | Pass | B |
| 10 | Gordon | Williamson | 50 | 80 | 76 | 69 | Pass | B |
| 11 | Clare | Stephen | 92 | 89 | 85 | 89 | Pass | A |
| 12 | Jack | Williamson | 74 | 68 | 78 | 73 | Pass | A |
| 13 | Ann | Shaw | 30 | 60 | 95 | 62 | Pass | B |
| 14 | Alison | Anderson | 82 | 86 | 90 | 86 | Pass | A |
| 15 | Jack | Anderson | 36 | 52 | 55 | 48 | Fail | Fail |
| 16 | Paul | Anderson | 45 | 59 | 52 | 52 | Pass | C |
| 17 | Bill | Andrews | 45 | 59 | 52 | 52 | Pass | C |
| 18 | John | Andrews | 77 | 80 | 99 | 85 | Pass | A |
| 19 | Gavin | Blair | 44 | 48 | 81 | 58 | Pass | C |
| 20 | Jill | Blair | 50 | 77 | 80 | 69 | Pass | B |

# 9.2 Sort

The data in your worksheet can be sorted into ascending or descending order. You can perform a simple sort, using the entries in one column only, or a more complex sort, sorting on up to three columns at a time.

When you sort your data, the block surrounding the current cell will be included in the sort – there should be no blank rows or columns inside the area you want to sort. Excel assumes that the first row of the data is a header row (with column labels) and doesn't include it in the sort.

**To perform a simple sort:**

**1** Select any cell in the column you want to sort on.

**2** Click the **Sort Ascending** [↑] or **Sort Descending** tool [↓] on the Standard toolbar.

Here is the student result worksheet sorted into descending order on the *Average Mark* column.

| | A | B | C | D | E | F | G | H |
|---|---|---|---|---|---|---|---|---|
| 1 | END OF TERM EXAM RESULTS | | | | | | | |
| 2 | | | | | | | | |
| 3 | Firstname | Surname | Computing % | Maths % | English % | Average Mark | Result | Grade |
| 4 | Clare | Stephen | 92 | 89 | 85 | 89 | Pass | A |
| 5 | Paul | Dunsire | 83 | 90 | 88 | 87 | Pass | A |
| 6 | Alison | Anderson | 82 | 06 | 90 | 86 | Pass | A |
| 7 | John | Andrews | 77 | 80 | 99 | 85 | Pass | A |
| 8 | David | Evans | 78 | 92 | 75 | 82 | Pass | A |
| 9 | Peter | Shaw | 77 | 82 | 80 | 80 | Pass | A |
| 10 | Peter | Johnston | 66 | 82 | 77 | 75 | Pass | A |
| 11 | Alison | Peterson | 75 | 65 | 82 | 74 | Pass | A |
| 12 | Gill | Ferguson | 80 | 76 | 66 | 74 | Pass | A |
| 13 | Jack | Williamson | 74 | 68 | 78 | 73 | Pass | A |
| 14 | Peter | Borthwick | 60 | 75 | 80 | 72 | Pass | A |
| 15 | Andrew | Borthwick | 50 | 88 | 74 | 71 | Pass | A |
| 16 | Kim | Stephen | 55 | 62 | 92 | 70 | Pass | B |
| 17 | Jill | Blair | 50 | 77 | 80 | 69 | Pass | B |
| 18 | Gordon | Williamson | 50 | 80 | 76 | 69 | Pass | B |
| 19 | Julie | Collins | 60 | 66 | 72 | 66 | Pass | B |
| 20 | Alison | Evans | 59 | 66 | 70 | 65 | Pass | B |

F4 = =AVERAGE(C4:E4)

**To perform a multi-level sort:**

1 Select any cell within the group of cells you want sorted.

2 Open the **Data** menu and choose **Sort...**

3 Select the main sort field from the **Sort by** list.

4 Choose the order – **Ascending** or **Descending**.

5 Select the second level sort field from the first **Then by** list, and set its sort order.

6 If necessary, set the third level sort options.

7 Click **OK**.

• Note that Excel assumes your list has a Header row – the one that normally contains the column labels or field names. If your list doesn't have a header row, i.e. you want the first row included in the sort, select the *No header row* option.

| | A | B | C | D | E | F | G | H |
|---|---|---|---|---|---|---|---|---|
| 1 | END OF TERM EXAM RESULTS | | | | | | | |
| 2 | | | | | | | | |
| 3 | Firstname | Surname | Computing % | Maths % | English % | Average Mark | Result | Grade |
| 4 | Alison | Anderson | 82 | 86 | 90 | 86 | Pass | A |
| 5 | Jack | Anderson | 36 | 52 | 55 | 48 | Fail | Fail |
| 6 | Paul | Anderson | 45 | 59 | 52 | 52 | Pass | C |
| 7 | Bill | Andrews | 45 | 59 | 52 | 52 | Pass | C |
| 8 | John | Andrews | 77 | 80 | 99 | 85 | Pass | A |
| 9 | Gavin | Blair | 44 | 48 | 81 | 58 | Pass | C |
| 10 | Jill | Blair | 50 | 77 | 80 | 69 | Pass | B |
| 11 | Andrew | Borthwick | 50 | 88 | 74 | 71 | Pass | A |
| 12 | Peter | Borthwick | 60 | 75 | 80 | 72 | Pass | A |
| 13 | Julie | Collins | 60 | 66 | 72 | 66 | Pass | B |
| 14 | Paul | Dunsire | 83 | 90 | 88 | 87 | Pass | A |
| 15 | Alison | Evans | 59 | 66 | 70 | 65 | Pass | B |
| 16 | David | Evans | 78 | 92 | 75 | 82 | Pass | A |
| 17 | Gill | Ferguson | 80 | 76 | 66 | 74 | Pass | A |
| 18 | Alexander | Johnston | 50 | 48 | 59 | 52 | Pass | C |
| 19 | Peter | Johnston | 66 | 82 | 77 | 75 | Pass | A |
| 20 | Gill | McLaren | 60 | 45 | 80 | 62 | Pass | B |

- The list in the previous example has been sorted into Surname order (ascending) then Firstname order (ascending).

You can also use the Sort feature to rearrange the columns in your worksheet. To do this, you must number the columns in the order you want them to go.

**To rearrange the columns:**

1 In the row immediately above (or below) your list, type in numbers to indicate the order you want the columns in.

2 Select any cell in the list you want to sort.

3 Open the **Data** menu and choose **Sort...**

4 Click **Options...**

5 Select **Sort left to right** in the Orientation options and click **OK**.

6 In the **Sort by** field, indicate the row number that has the entries you want to sort (row 3 in this example).

| | A | B | C | D | E | F | G | H |
|---|---|---|---|---|---|---|---|---|
| 1 | END OF TERM EXAM RESULTS | | | | | | | |
| 2 | | | | | | | | |
| 3 | 2 | 1 | 3 | 4 | 5 | 6 | 7 | 8 |
| 4 | Firstname | Surname | Computing % | Maths % | English % | Average Mark | Result | Grade |
| 5 | Alison | Anderson | 82 | 86 | 90 | 86 | Pass | A |
| 6 | Jack | Anderson | 36 | 52 | 55 | 48 | Fail | Fail |
| 7 | Paul | Anderson | 45 | 59 | 52 | 52 | Pass | C |
| 8 | Bill | Andrews | 45 | 59 | 52 | 52 | Pass | C |
| 9 | John | Andrews | 77 | 80 | 99 | 85 | Pass | A |
| 10 | Gavin | Blair | 44 | 48 | 81 | 58 | Pass | C |
| 11 | Jill | Blair | 50 | 77 | 80 | 69 | Pass | B |
| 12 | Andrew | Borthwick | 50 | 88 | 74 | 71 | Pass | A |
| 13 | Peter | Borthwick | 60 | 75 | 80 | 72 | Pass | A |
| 14 | Julie | Collins | 60 | 66 | 72 | 66 | Pass | B |
| 15 | Paul | Dunsire | 83 | 90 | 88 | 87 | Pass | A |
| 16 | Alison | Evans | 59 | 66 | 70 | 65 | Pass | B |
| 17 | David | Evans | 78 | 92 | 75 | 82 | Pass | A |
| 18 | Gill | Ferguson | 80 | 76 | 66 | 74 | Pass | A |
| 19 | Alexander | Johnston | 50 | 48 | 59 | 52 | Pass | C |
| 20 | Peter | Johnston | 66 | 82 | 77 | 75 | Pass | A |

7 Click **OK**.

- Once your data has been sorted, you can delete the row that contains the numbers.

Columns rearranged in order of the numbers in Row 3

## Circular references

If you try to sort columns that have formulas in them, you may run into problems with circular references where a formula in a cell points to the cell itself. If this occurs, edit the formula. If you create a circular reference, Excel will warn you and ask what you want to do about it (see section 5.6).

# 9.3 AutoFilter

You may want to display only the records from your list that meet specific criteria. The AutoFilter can quickly filter out the un-wanted records and display only those that meet your criteria.

**To switch the AutoFilter on:**

**1** Select a cell within the list you want to work with.

**2** Open the **Data** menu, choose **Filter**, then **AutoFilter**.

• Each field name (column heading) becomes a combo box (drop-down list), with a drop-down arrow to its right.

**To view records that contain a specific value:**

**1** Click the drop-down arrow to the right of the field name you want to select on.

**2** Select the value you want to view the records for.

**3** If you want to filter the result further, based on a value in another column, repeat steps **1** and **2** on the other column.

In this example, the students who have an A in the Grade column have been selected.

The column or columns that you have specified your criteria in have a blue arrow to the right of the field name so you can identify which columns have conditions set in them.

- By default, AutoFilter will list records that are equal to the criteria you have selected. If you want a different operator, e.g. *Does not equal*, you must use the **Custom AutoFilter** dialog box. To open the dialog box, choose **Custom...** from the drop-down list.

**To display all the records again:**

**1** Click the drop-down arrow on the column(s) that have criteria set.

**2** Choose **All** from the list of options.

Or

**1** Open the **Data** menu and select **Filter**.

**2** Choose **Show All**.

You can use AutoFilter to filter a list by up to two values in the same column. To do so you must set up a Custom filter.

**To filter a list by two values in the same column:**

**1** Click the drop-down arrow to the right of the field name you want to select on.

**2** Select **Custom...**

**3** At the **Custom AutoFilter** dialog box, set up the criteria required – in this case we are looking for students who have either a C grade or a Fail.

**4** Click **OK**.

---

**Custom AutoFilter** ☒

Show rows where:
Grade

| equals | ✔ | | C | ✔ |

    ○ And  ⊙ Or

| equals | ✔ | | Fail | ✔ |

Use ? to represent any single character
Use * to represent any series of characters

        [ OK ]  [ Cancel ]

---

◆ The list of records matching your criteria will be displayed.

If you want to list all students who have more than a certain score in the *Average Mark* column, you must use the Custom AutoFilter, e.g. *Average Mark is greater than 55*. If you want all students whose surname falls within the range M–S (*Surname is greater than L*, and *Surname is less than T*), you must use the Custom AutoFilter.

**To switch AutoFilter off:**

**1** Open the **Data** menu.

**2** Choose **Filter**, then **AutoFilter** to toggle the filter off.

# 9.4 Advanced Filter

If you want to use several criteria to filter your data, or if you want to keep a set of criteria for future use, you must use the Advanced Filter. This requires you to specify the criteria you wish to apply on a separate area of the worksheet. The criteria in this range are then applied to your list of data.

Set up your criteria range first, then apply it to the list of data.

**To set up the criteria range:**

**1** Copy the column headings or field names to a blank area in your worksheet.

**2** Specify the criteria required in the rows under the copied column headings.

♦ If you enter several conditions in one row, Excel will only return a record where the first and the second and the third condition, etc. are met – in other words ALL the conditions must be met in a single record before a record is returned.

♦ If you enter the conditions in different rows, Excel will return a record that meets one condition or the other.

The screenshot below gives examples of valid criteria.

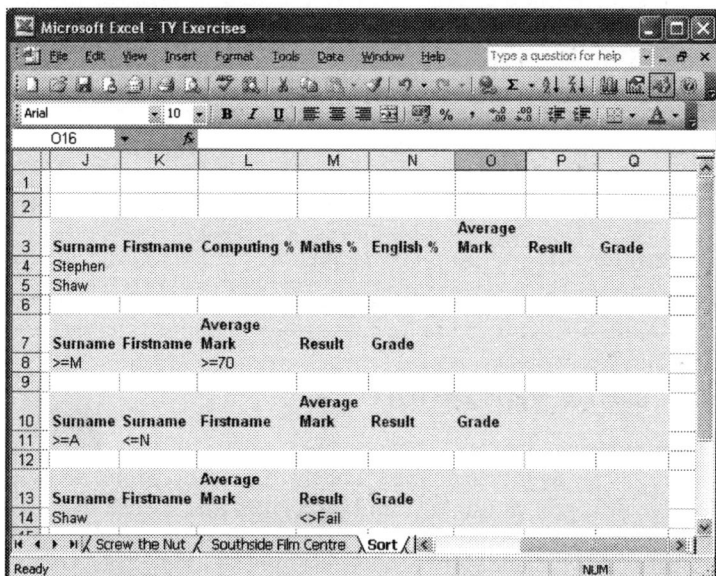

- The first one will list only those who have the surname Stephen OR Shaw.

- The second one will list all whose surname falls between M and the end of the alphabet, AND have 70 or more in the Average column.

- The third one lists all whose surname starts with a letter between A and N.

- The fourth one lists all the Shaws who have not failed.

**To apply the conditions set in the criteria range:**

1 Select any cell in the list you want to extract records from.

2 From the **Data** menu choose **Filter**, then **Advanced Filter**.

3 Do you want to filter the list in place, or copy the records that match the criteria to a separate area of the worksheet – select the option required.

4 Specify the range you want to extract records from (Excel should suggest the range you have selected a cell in – correct the range if necessary).

5 Indicate the cells that hold the field names and the criteria to apply. Do not include any blank rows in the criteria area.

6 If you want the result in a different location from the original list, give the cell reference of the top left corner of the area you want the result to appear in the **Copy to:** field.

7 Click **OK**.

**If you filtered the list in place, to display all the records again:**

- Open the **Data** menu, choose **Filter** then select **Show All**.

# 9.5 Data validation

When entering data into a worksheet, you will want to try to ensure, as far as is practicable, that the data is accurate. To help achieve this, you can set up validation rules for any cell or range of cells where you want to check the validity of the data entered.

By default, each cell in a worksheet will accept any value. However, you can limit the range of acceptable entries by setting up validation rules. In our *Student Results*, we could set a rule for the data area in the *Subject* columns so they would accept values between 0 and 100 only. Anything over 100 or less than 0, would not be accepted and an error message would appear.

## To set a validation rule:

**1** Select the cell or cells you want the rule to apply to (do not include the column heading or any other cells).

**2** Open the **Data** menu and choose **Validation...**

**3** On the **Settings** tab, complete the validation criteria fields.

Type of data ⟶

Match style ⟶

Values to match ⟶

**4** If you want a message displayed when the cell is selected, enter it on the **Input Message** tab.

**5** If you want a specific message to appear when the rule is not met, enter it on the **Error Alert** tab (a default message appears if you don't set up your own).

**6** Click **OK** when you're finished.

• When you select a cell that has the validation rule applied to it, the input message will be displayed.

• If you enter invalid data into a cell that has a validation rule applied to it, the message you set up on the **Error Alert** tab (or the default Error Alert message) will appear.

**To remove a validation rule from your cells:**

**1** Select the cell or cells you want to remove the rule from.

**2** Open the **Data** menu and choose **Validation...**

**3** Click the **Clear All** button.

**4** Click **OK**.

## 9.6 Data form

As an alternative to displaying the data in your worksheet as a list, you may find a form easier to work with. A form displays one record, or row, from your list at a time, rather than as many records as will fit on your screen.

**To display your data in a form:**

**1** Select any cell in the list of data you want to display in a form.

**2** Open the **Data** menu and choose **Form...**

The first record in the list of data will be displayed.

Fields that you can enter data into or edit are displayed as Text Boxes – *Firstname, Surname* and *Subject Marks* in this example.

Calculated fields have their value displayed, but you cannot enter or edit the entry in them directly.

**Sort**

| | | 1 of 25 |
|---|---|---|
| S<u>u</u>rname: | Anderson | New |
| F<u>i</u>rstname: | Alison | <u>D</u>elete |
| C<u>o</u>mputing %: | 82 | Restore |
| <u>M</u>aths %: | 86 | |
| <u>E</u>nglish %: | 90 | Find <u>P</u>rev |
| <u>A</u>verage Mark: | 86 | Find <u>N</u>ext |
| Res<u>u</u>lt: | Pass | <u>C</u>riteria |
| G<u>r</u>ade: | A | Cl<u>o</u>se |

**To add a new record:**

♦ Click the **New** button and complete the blank form – the data will be saved on the sheet for you.

**To delete a record:**

♦ Display the record you want to delete and click the **Delete** button. Confirm the deletion at the prompt if you are sure that you want to go ahead and remove the record.

If you edit the contents of a field, then realize that you shouldn't have, you can restore the fields to recover the data that they contained when you accessed the record. This only works if you have *not* left the record. If you make changes, go to another record, then go back to the record you edited, you will have to manually update the fields again.

**To restore a record:**

♦ Click the **Restore** button on the form.

**To move from one record to another:**

♦ Click the **Find Prev** or **Find Next** buttons to move back and forward through the records.

**To display records that meet specific criteria:**

**1** Click the **Criteria** button on the form.

**2** Complete the fields with the criteria you want to apply.

**3** Use **Find Prev** or **Find Next** to move through the records that meet the criteria specified.

To cancel the criteria:

1 Display the **Criteria**.

2 Click **Clear**.

3 Click the **Form** button to leave the **Criteria** dialog box.

To return to your worksheet:

• Click the **Close** button.

| Sort | | |
|---|---|---|
| Surname: | | Criteria |
| Firstname: | | New |
| Computing %: | | Clear |
| Maths %: | | Restore |
| English %: | | |
| Average Mark: | >=65 | Find Prev |
| Result: | | Find Next |
| Grade: | | Form |
| | | Close |

## 9.7 Subtotals

Lists of data can easily be summarized automatically using subtotals. In this example, customers buy flowers from a garden centre. The centre wants to know the total value of orders from each customer over the period. This is calculated in Column G.

To display subtotals:

1 Sort the data into ascending order on the field that you want to create subtotals after, e.g. *Customer*.

| | A | B | C | D | E | F | G | H | I | J |
|---|---|---|---|---|---|---|---|---|---|---|
| 1 | | **Gerry's Garden Centre** | | | | | | | **Prices each** | |
| 2 | | | | | | | | | Roses £ | 1.00 |
| 3 | Order Summary for | December | | | | | | | Lilies £ | 1.50 |
| 4 | | | | | | | | | Carnations £ | 0.50 |
| 5 | Order ID | Date | Customer | Roses | Lilies | Carnations | Total Cost | | | |
| 6 | FF100 | 01/12/2003 | Fabby Flowers | 30 | 10 | 20 | £ 55.00 | | | |
| 7 | GT001 | 03/12/2003 | Golden Tulip | 20 | 20 | 40 | £ 70.00 | | | |
| 8 | AF001 | 03/12/2003 | Amy's Flowers | 50 | 60 | 80 | £ 180.00 | | | |
| 9 | FF101 | 04/12/2003 | Fabby Flowers | 22 | 10 | 50 | £ 62.00 | | | |
| 10 | AF002 | 04/12/2003 | Amy's Flowers | 60 | 30 | 20 | £ 115.00 | | | |
| 11 | GT002 | 06/12/2003 | Golden Tulip | 16 | 22 | 30 | £ 64.00 | | | |
| 12 | BB001 | 06/12/2003 | Best Blooms | 10 | 20 | 30 | £ 55.00 | | | |
| 13 | GT003 | 07/12/2003 | Golden Tulip | 20 | 18 | 30 | £ 62.00 | | | |
| 14 | AF003 | 07/12/2003 | Amy's Flowers | 60 | 50 | 90 | £ 180.00 | | | |
| 15 | FF102 | 08/12/2003 | Fabby Flowers | 16 | 20 | 30 | £ 61.00 | | | |
| 16 | GT004 | 08/12/2002 | Golden Tulip | 20 | 24 | 30 | £ 71.00 | | | |
| 17 | FF103 | 10/12/2003 | Fabby Flowers | 18 | 22 | 50 | £ 76.00 | | | |
| 18 | BB002 | 10/12/2003 | Best Blooms | 20 | 20 | 20 | £ 60.00 | | | |
| 19 | GT005 | 11/12/2003 | Golden Tulip | 14 | 20 | 70 | £ 79.00 | | | |
| 20 | GT006 | 12/12/2002 | Golden Tulip | 14 | 16 | 60 | £ 68.00 | | | |
| 21 | FF104 | 15/12/2003 | Fabby Flowers | 16 | 20 | 80 | £ 86.00 | | | |
| 22 | BB003 | 15/12/2003 | Best Blooms | 30 | 50 | 70 | £ 140.00 | | | |
| 23 | GT006 | 16/12/2003 | Golden Tulip | 20 | 30 | 50 | £ 90.00 | | | |

**2** Select any cell within the data you wish to create subtotals for.

**3** Open the **Data** menu and choose **Subtotals**.

**4** In the **At each change in:** field, select the item you wish to subtotal on – *Customer* in this example.

**5** Select the function required from the **Use function:** list (**Sum** if you want subtotals).

**6** In the **Add subtotal to:** list tick the box to indicate where you want the subtotal displayed.

**7** Select/deselect the checkboxes as required.

**8** Click **OK**.

The result is a list showing the data grouped and subtotalled as requested.

The outline pane on the left can be used to expand and collapse the level of detail required. In the example here, Level 1 = Grand Total, Level 2 = Item Subtotal, Level 3 = Detail.

You can display the amount of detail required by clicking the level numbers at the top of the pane.

- You can collapse and expand individual groups within the

list by clicking the Hide ▬ and Show ▬ buttons in the outline pane.

• You can show/hide the outline with the command **Data > Group and Outline > Clear Outline/Auto Outline**.

# 9.8 Database functions

## DCOUNT

DCOUNT looks at a list of values, finds the rows that satisfy specific criteria, and counts them. It is used when you want to count the values that match **>1** criteria.

Set up a criteria range – see section 9.4, *Advanced Filter*.

**To insert the DCOUNT function:**

**1** Select the cell that you want the answer to appear in.

**2** Click the **Insert Function** button and choose **DCOUNT** from the function lists.

**3** Enter the range of cells that your list of data fills in the **Database** field.

**4** For the **Field,** enter a column label or number that you want Excel to base its count on (this must be a numeric column).

**5** Specify the range that the **Criteria** are in.

**6** Click **OK**.

## DSUM, DMIN, DMAX

Other functions that work along the same principle are DSUM, DMIN and DMAX. In this example, Excel is used to keep details of orders for cut flowers from shops. Summary data could be produced using the database functions. Experiment with these (following the steps as for DCOUNT, but substituting the appropriate function) to produce summary data.

## Summary

In this chapter we have discussed:

- Database terminology and how it relates to Excel terminology
- Sorting rows into ascending or descending order
- Multi-level sorts
- Using Sort to rearrange columns
- Locating data using the AutoFilter
- Locating data using the Advanced Filter
- Validation rules
- Displaying your list as a simple form
- Subtotals
- Database functions

# 10

## macros

**In this chapter you will learn:**

- what macros are
- how to record, run, edit and delete macros
- about making your macros available to all workbooks

## Aims of this chapter

We have already discussed some of the features that can be used to help you automate the way you work in Excel – AutoFormat, Styles, Templates, etc. In this chapter we will consider how macros can help you automate your work. Macros are useful when you want to automate a routine that you perform regularly. We will look at some examples where you may find macros useful. You will learn how to record, play back and edit the macros you create.

# 10.1 What are macros?

A macro is a set of Excel commands grouped together so that you can execute them as a single command.

If you perform a task often, but cannot find an Excel keyboard shortcut, or tool, that runs through the sequence you want to use, you should record the commands into a macro. You have then created a 'custom' command.

## What could you use a macro for?

* Speeding up routine editing and formatting.
* Recording the instructions to create a new document using one of your own templates, e.g. your budget or monthly sales figures.
* Quickly accessing an option in a dialog box that you regularly use.
* Combining a group of commands you often execute in the same sequence.

There are two ways to create macros in Excel:

* **Recording** – we will be using this option. You can record any function that you can access through the menus and dialog boxes.
* **Visual Basic Editor** – you can record powerful, flexible macros using this. These macros can include Visual Basic as well as Excel commands. We will take a brief excursion into the Editor when we discuss editing macros.

## 10.2 Recording your macro

Before you start recording your macro, think through what it is that you want to record. If there are any commands that you're not sure about, try them out first to check that they do what you want to record.

Try recording a simple macro that wil create a new workbook using one of your own templates.

To *create* your *new* workbook, you must:

1 Choose New from the File menu.

2 Click *On* My Computer... on the New Workbook Task Pane.

3 Select your template from the General tab.

4 Click OK.

The next example uses the template set up in Chapter 8.

To record *the* macro:

1 Open the Tools menu, choose Macro then Record New Macro...

2 Give your macro a name, e.g. *MyTemplate*.

• Don't use spaces in the macro name – most of the punctuation characters are also not allowed. If you want to separate words, use the underline character.

3 If you want a keyboard shortcut, click in the Shortcut field and enter the shortcut you want to use, e.g. *Ctrl+Shift+T*.

4 Select the workbook you want to store the macro in.

• If you choose the Personal Macro Workbook, your macro will be globally available, in every workbook you create.

5 Click OK.

- You will be returned to your worksheet, and the *Stop Recording* toolbar will be displayed.

**6** Work through the steps you want to record.

**7** Click the *Stop* tool on the Stop Recording toolbar when you've finished.

- If the Stop Recording toolbar is not displayed, you can stop by opening the **Tools** menu, choosing **Macro** and then *Stop Recording*.

## 10.3 Playing back your macro

You can play back a macro with the keyboard shortcut, if you created one, or through the Tools menu.

**To use the keyboard shortcut:**

- Press the keyboard shortcut key sequence you recorded, e.g. **Ctrl+Shift+T** to create your new workbook.

**To use the Tools menu:**

**1** Open the **Tools** menu and choose **Macro**.

**2** Select **Macros...**

**3** At the **Macro** dialog box, select the macro you want to play back and click **Run**.

This simple example illustrates how a macro can be recorded and executed. You will find that macros are especially useful when you have long sequences of commands to work through.

# 10.4 Ideas for more macros

You can record almost anything you want into a macro. Some of the things that you could record into a macro may also be automated in other ways, e.g. AutoFormat or Styles. Macros are usually used to carry out a sequence of commands.

If you find that you regularly use a series of commands in the same order, or use an option that is buried deep in a dialog box, macros can help you speed up the way you work.

Try out the following macros to get some more practice. They are all easy to set up.

## Setting up a Header and/or Footer

If you use the same header and/or footer in many of your workbooks, you could record the sequence of commands into a macro.

1  Open the **Tools** menu, choose **Macro** then **Record New Macro…**

2  Give your macro a name – *HeaderFooter* or something similar.

3  If you want a keyboard shortcut, click in the *Shortcut* field and enter the shortcut, e.g. **Ctrl+Shift+F**.

4  Select the workbook you want to store the macro in – store it in the Personal Macro Workbook if you want it to be available to all workbooks.

5  Click **OK**. You will be returned to your worksheet, and the Stop Recording toolbar will be displayed.

6  Open the **File** menu and choose **Page Setup…**

7  Select the **Header/Footer** tab.

8  Set up the header and/or footer as required.

9  Click **OK**.

10  Click the *Stop* tool when you've finished.

## Discount calculator

Let's say you offer a discount to your customers based on the amount of their order. You could record a simple discount calculator into a macro, then access the calculator from any workbook. This macro will:

1  Create a new blank worksheet within your workbook.

2  Enter the text and formula to the discount calculator.

3  Protect the sheet so that only the *Amount of Order* details can be entered.

Try it out!

1  Create a new workbook, or open an existing one.

2  Start to record a new macro.

3  Give your macro a name – *DiscountCal* or something similar – and enter a keyboard shortcut if you want one.

4  Select the workbook you want to store the macro in.

5  Click *OK*.

6  Insert a new worksheet – open the *Insert* menu and choose **Work**sheet.

7  Enter the text and the formula to calculate the discount (in this example 7.5%) and balance due (see below – don't display the formulas).

8  Format the cells to *Currency*.

9  Unlock the cell that will take the *Amount of order* and protect the worksheet (see section 5.9).

**10** Stop recording.

If you recorded the macro in your Personal Macro Workbook, you can access it from anywhere using the keyboard shortcut, or run the macro from the Macro dialog box.

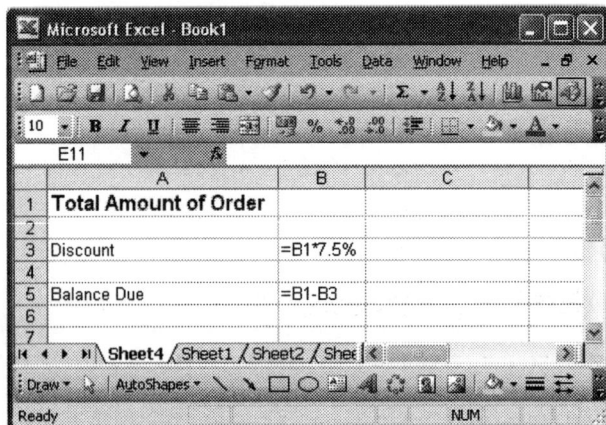

## 10.5 Deleting a macro

As you experiment with setting up macros, you will inevitably end up with some that you don't want to keep. They may not prove as useful as you first thought, or they might not run properly. You can delete any macro you no longer require.

If the macro you want to delete is in the Personal Macro Workbook, you must 'unhide' the workbook before you can delete it.

**To unhide the Personal Macro Workbook:**

**1** Open the **Window** menu and choose **Unhide...**

**2** Select the workbook – *Personal* in this case.

**3** Click **OK**.

**To delete a macro:**

**1** Open the **Tools** menu and select **Macro**.

**2** Choose **Macros...**

**3** Select the macro you want to delete from the list displayed.

**4** Click **Delete**.

**5** Confirm the deletion at the prompt.

If you have displayed your Personal Macro Workbook, you must hide it again once you've deleted any macros you don't want to keep. Do not close it – if you do you won't be able to use the macros that you recorded in the workbook.

**To hide the Personal Macro Workbook again:**

♦ Open the **Window** menu and choose **Hide**.

## 10.6 Editing a macro

I'd suggest you re-record any short macro that has an error in it rather than try to edit it – it will probably be quicker. However, if you have recorded a longer macro or have a minor adjustment

to make, it may be quicker to edit it rather than re-record the whole thing.

The macros you record are translated into Visual Basic – so things may look a bit strange when you first try editing a macro. But don't worry – if you take your time and have a look through the instructions you'll soon be able to relate your actions in Excel to the Visual Basic code.

When editing a macro, be very careful not to delete anything you don't understand, or insert anything that should not be there – you might find your macro no longer runs properly if you do. If the worst comes to the worst and the macro stops working, you can always record it again.

The Visual Basic code will often have far more lines of code than the number of commands you intentionally recorded. Don't worry about this – some instructions are picked up from default settings in dialog boxes. Just scroll through until you see something you recognize as the line you want to change.

Let's try editing the discount amount in our discount calculator to make it 12.5%.

If the discount calculator macro is in the Personal Macro Workbook, you must unhide the workbook before you can edit it.

**To *edit the* macro:**

**1** Open the **Tools** menu and choose **Macro** then **Macros...**

**2** Select the macro you wish to edit.

**3** Click the E*dit* button.

◆ The Visual Basic code for the macro will be displayed.

**4** Scroll through the code to find the area you want to change.

**5** Edit as required.

**6** Save the changes – click the S*ave* tool on the Standard toolbar.

**7** Close – click the C*lose* button on the Microsoft Visual Basic title bar.

# 10.7 Saving macros on exit

If you have saved some macros into your Personal Macro Workbook, a prompt will appear when you exit Excel, asking if you want to save the changes to that workbook. If you want to be able to use the macros you have created the next time you use Excel, click *Yes* or *Yes To All* at the prompt.

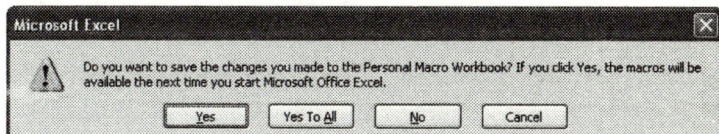

```
Microsoft Excel                                                    ✕
  ⚠   Do you want to save the changes you made to the Personal Macro Workbook? If you click Yes, the macros will be
      available the next time you start Microsoft Office Excel.
            [ Yes ]    [ Yes To All ]    [ No ]    [ Cancel ]
```

---

## Summary

In this chapter we have discussed:

◆ **The Macro Recorder**

◆ **Keyboard shortcut for macros**

◆ **Running a macro**

◆ **Deleting a macro**

◆ **Editing a macro using the Visual Basic Editor**

◆ **Saving the changes to the Personal Macro Workbook so that you can use them again the next time you use Excel**

# toolbars

## In this chapter you will learn:

- about working with toolbars
- how to manipulate and customize toolbars
- how to assign macros to tools

**Aims of this chapter**

In this chapter we'll look at basic toolbar manipulation – the positioning of toolbars, and showing and hiding them. We'll also discuss how you can edit toolbars, create new ones and assign macros to them. Finally, we'll discuss some of the other options available when working with toolbars.

# 11.1 Standard and Formatting toolbars

When working in Excel the Standard toolbar and Formatting toolbar normally share a row along the top of your screen. If you prefer to give these toolbars a row each, you can switch the row-sharing option off.

**To toggle row-sharing for the Standard and Formatting toolbar:**

• Click the Toolbar Options button (drop-down arrow at right edge of toolbar) and click **Show Buttons on One Row/Show Buttons on Two Rows**

Or

**1** Right-click on a toolbar.

**2** Choose **Customize...** from the list.

**3** Select the **Options** tab.

**4** Select or deselect **Show Standard and Formatting toolbars on two rows.**

Customize

| Toolbars | Commands | Options |

Personalized Menus and Toolbars

☑ Show Standard and Formatting toolbars on two rows
☐ Always show full menus
    ☑ Show full menus after a short delay

[ Reset menu and toolbar usage data ]

Other

☐ Large icons
☑ List font names in their font
☑ Show ScreenTips on toolbars

Menu animations: (System default) ▾

[ Close ]

Other options on this tab let you control how the menus work

If you have the Standard and Formatting toolbars sharing one row, there isn't much room to display all of their tools.

**To access a tool that is not displayed on the toolbar:**

**1** Display the tools by clicking the **Toolbar Options** drop-down arrow at the end of the toolbar.

**2** Click on the tool required.

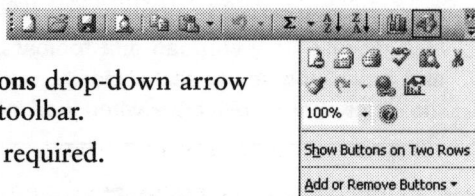

## 11.2 Moving toolbars

Toolbars can be positioned *anywhere* on your screen. There are four *docking* areas – at the top, bottom, left and right of the Excel window. You can also leave your toolbar *floating* anywhere on the screen.

**To move a toolbar if it is docked:**

**1** Point to the dotted line at the left edge of the toolbar (if it is docked at the top or bottom of the screen) or top edge (if it is docked at the left or right).

**2** Drag and drop the toolbar into its new position.

**To move a toolbar if it is not docked:**

**1** Point to its Title bar.

**2** Drag and drop the toolbar into its new position.

## 11.3 Showing and hiding toolbars

You will have noticed that some toolbars appear and disappear automatically when you are working in Excel. You can also opt to show or hide toolbars whenever you wish. Provided you have at least one toolbar displayed, you can use the shortcut method to show or hide toolbars.

**To use the shortcut method:**

**1** Point to a toolbar.

**2** Click the *right* mouse button.

**♦** Any toolbars that are already displayed have a tick beside their name.

**3** Click (using the *left* mouse button) on the toolbar name that you wish to show or hide.

If no toolbars are displayed, you must use the **View** menu to show them again.

**1** Open the **View** menu and choose **Toolbars**.

**2** Click on the one you want to show.

Using either of the methods above, you can show or hide one toolbar at a time. If you want to change the display status of several toolbars at the one time, it may be quicker to use the **Customize** dialog box.

**1** Right-click on any open toolbar.

Or

♦ Open the **View** menu and choose **Toolbars**.

**2** Click **Customize...**

**3** Select or deselect the toolbars in the list as required.

**4** Click **Close**.

| | |
|---|---|
| ✓ | Standard |
| ✓ | Formatting |
| | Borders |
| | Chart |
| | Control Toolbox |
| ✓ | Drawing |
| | External Data |
| | Forms |
| | Formula Auditing |
| | List |
| | Picture |
| | PivotTable |
| | Protection |
| | Reviewing |
| | Task Pane |
| | Text To Speech |
| | Visual Basic |
| | Watch Window |
| | Web |
| | WordArt |
| | Customize... |

Toolbars are useful, but the more you have open, the less you can see of your sheet!

# 11.4 Editing existing toolbars

If you find that there are some tools on a toolbar that you tend not to use, or if you want to add another tool to a toolbar, you can edit the toolbar. If you want to add several tools to a toolbar, you should create a new toolbar and add your tools to it – see section 11.5. If you want to edit a toolbar it must be displayed.

**To edit an existing toolbar:**

1 Display the toolbar you want to edit.

2 Click the **Toolbar Options** drop-down arrow to the right of the toolbar.

3 Place the mouse pointer over **Add or Remove Buttons**.

4 Point to the toolbar name.

5 Select or deselect the tools as required.

Or

• If the tool is not displayed, click **Customize** to open the **Customize** dialog box.

6 Select the **Commands** tab.

| | | |
|---|---|---|
| Standard | ▶ | |
| Formatting | ▶ | |
| Customize... | | |

New
Open
Save
Permission (Unrestricted Access)
Mail Recipient
Print (Document Image Writer)
Print Preview
Spelling...
Research...
Cut
Copy
Paste
Format Painter
Undo
Redo
Hyperlink...
AutoSum
Sort Ascending
Sort Descending
Chart Wizard
Default Chart
Drawing
Zoom:
Microsoft Excel Help          F1
PivotTable and PivotChart Report...
Comment
AutoFilter
Reset Toolbar

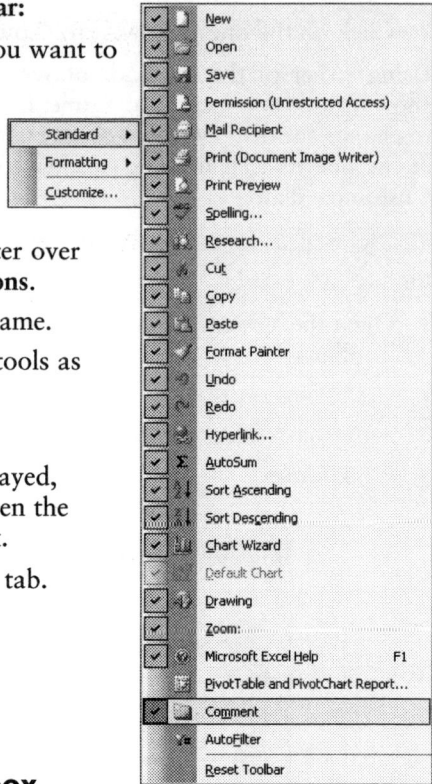

## Customize dialog box

The Customize dialog box can be opened from the Add or Remove Buttons list in the Toolbar Options (see above), or from the bottom of the Toolbar list displayed when you right-click on a toolbar or choose Toolbars from the View menu.

You can add tools to, delete them from and move them on a toolbar when the dialog box is open.

• Select the **Commands** tab in the **Customize** dialog box.

**To add a tool:**

**1** Select the **Category** of tool you're looking for.

**2** Locate the tool in the **Commands** list.

**3** Drag it over to the toolbar – a very dark I-beam with a **+** by its side shows where it will go – and drop it into position (if you are not over a toolbar, the mouse pointer has a small button with an **x**).

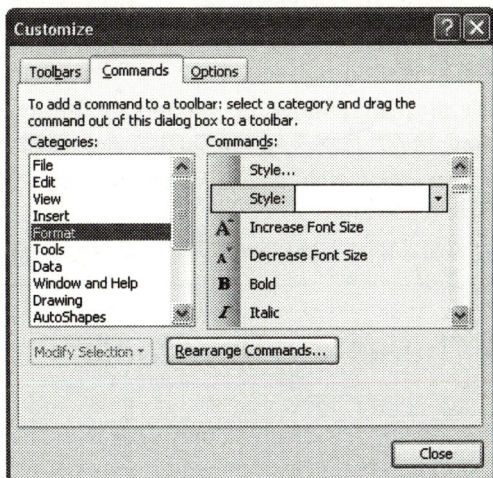

**To move a tool:**

**1** With the **Customize** dialog box open, drag the tool to the correct position on the toolbar.

**2** Drop it.

**To remove a tool:**

**1** With the **Customize** dialog box open, drag the tool off the toolbar.

**2** Drop it anywhere.

**3** Click **Close** in the **Customize** dialog box when you've finished editing your toolbar.

The drop-down list tools that appear on toolbars, e.g. Style and Font on the Formatting toolbar take up a lot more room than one of the smaller buttons.

If you need to free up some space on a toolbar that contains drop-down tools, you can change the size of these tools.

**To change the size of a drop-down tool:**

1 Open the **Customize** dialog box.

2 On the appropriate toolbar, select the tool you want to resize e.g. | Normal ▾ |.

3 Click and drag the right or left edge of it – the mouse pointer becomes a thick double-headed arrow when you are in the correct place.

---

**Shortcut**

You can quickly move or delete tools from a displayed toolbar *without* opening the Customize dialog box.

*To move a tool:* Hold down [Alt] and drag the tool along the toolbar (or to another toolbar).

*To delete a tool:* Hold down [Alt] and drag it off the toolbar.

---

# 11.5 Creating a new toolbar

If you have several tools that you'd like to add to a toolbar (or macros to assign to tools), you may need to create a new toolbar, rather than try to squeeze tools into the existing ones.

**To create a new toolbar:**

1 Open the **Customize** dialog box.

2 Select the **Toolbars** tab.

3 Click **New…**

4 Give your toolbar a name and click **OK**.

5 Your toolbar will be displayed.

6 Choose the **Commands** tab and add the tools you require to your new toolbar (see section 11.4).

7 Close the **Customize** dialog box.

# 11.6 Adding your macros to toolbars

In Chapter 10 we discussed macros. The ones you set up can be assigned to a tool on a toolbar, and run with a simple click.

**To assign a macro to a toolbar:**

1 Display the toolbar you want to assign your macro to.

2 Open the **Customize** dialog box.

3 Choose the **Commands** tab.

4 Select the **Macros** category.

5 Drag the Custom Button onto your toolbar.

6 Right-click on the tool and click **Assign Macro...**

7 Select the macro you want to assign to the macro button.

8 Click **OK**.

9 Close the **Customize** dialog box.

# 11.7 Change a button image and name

You may want to change the custom button image – things get a bit confusing if you use the same one for several macros. If you are assigning several macros to tools on a toolbar, you don't want them all with a smiley face!

**To change the button image:**

1 Display the toolbar that has the macro button image on it.
2 Open the **Customize** dialog box and select the **Commands** tab.
3 Select the macro button on your toolbar.
4 Click **Modify Selection**.
5 Choose **Change Button Image**.
6 Select an image for your macro button.

The screen tip that appears when you point to a custom button is taken from the **Name** field in the **Modify Selection** list.

**To create a screen tip:**

1 Follow steps 1 to 4 as above.
2 Select the text '*&Custom Button*' that appears in the **Name:** field.
3 Type in the text you want to display.
4 Click anywhere off the list to close it.
5 Close the **Customize** dialog box when you've finished.

| |
|---|
| Reset |
| Delete |
| Name: My Template |
| Copy Button Image |
| Paste Button Image |
| Reset Button Image |
| Edit Button Image... |
| Change Button Image ▶ |
| ✔ Default Style |
| Text Only (Always) |
| Text Only (in Menus) |
| Image and Text |
| Begin a Group |
| Assign Hyperlink ▶ |
| Assign Macro... |
| Modify Selection ▾ |

# 11.8 Resetting toolbars

If you have modified one of the preset toolbars that come with Excel, then decide you want to set it back to how it was when you installed the package, you can restore its original settings.

**To reset an Excel toolbar:**

1 Click **Reset Toolbar** at the bottom of the **Add or Remove Buttons** list.

Or

**2** Open the **Customize** dialog box and select the **Toolbars** tab.

**3** Click on the toolbar you want to reset – it doesn't matter if the toolbar is displayed or not.

**4** Click the **Reset...** button.

**5** Respond to the prompt as appropriate – **OK** to reset the toolbar, **Cancel** if you've changed your mind.

# Summary

In this chapter we have discussed:

- Positioning toolbars on your screen
- Showing and hiding toolbars
- Adding tools to toolbars
- Moving tools on toolbars
- Removing tools from toolbars
- Creating new toolbars
- Assigning macros to a toolbar
- Changing the custom button image and name
- Resetting an Excel toolbar

# 12

# excel with other applications

**In this chapter you will learn:**

- the difference between linking and embedding
- how to link data in other applications to Excel
- how to use Excel data in a Word Mail Merge

## Aims of this chapter

Excel is part of Microsoft Office and integrates very well with the other applications in the suite. If you have the full suite then you have the benefit of being able to use the most appropriate tool for the job. This chapter discusses some ways in which the Office applications can be integrated.

# 12.1 Linking vs embedding

Linking and embedding are two techniques that enable you to exchange data between Excel and other applications. The key differences between linked and embedded data lie in where it is stored and how it is updated.

## Linked data

Linked data *is not* stored in your Excel workbook. It is stored in a file, e.g. a document or presentation, in the source application (the one in which it was created). The data is updated within the source application – and those changes are reflected in the Excel workbook to which it is linked.

**Advantages of linking data include:**

* The Excel workbook is smaller than with embedded data.
* The data in the Excel workbook reflects the current status of the source data.

## Embedded data

Embedded data *is* stored in your Excel workbook. However, when you create and edit the data, you have access to all the functions within the source application.

**Advantages of embedding data:**

* All the data is held in one file.
* You have access to powerful functions that are not part of the Excel application when creating and editing the object.

The following sections discuss some of the methods you can use to integrate the data across the applications in Office.

## 12.2 Copy and Paste

You can copy text, data, graphics, charts, etc. from one application to another within the Office suite using simple copy and paste techniques. We will consider how you can copy charts and data *from* Excel into other applications in the Office suite.

**To copy and paste:**

**1** Start Excel *and* the application you want to copy the data or chart to.

**2** Open the workbook that you are copying from, and the file that will receive the copy.

**3** Select the chart or data you want to copy.

**4** Click the **Copy** tool 📋 on the Standard toolbar.

**5** Switch to the application you want to copy the data or chart into.

**6** Place the insertion point where you want the data or chart to appear.

**7** Click the **Paste** tool 📋 on the Standard toolbar.

When you copy charts and data in this way, the chart or data is not 'linked' to the original data in the Excel workbook in any way. Should you edit the data in Excel, the data you copied into the destination file remains as it was when you copied it.

You can copy and paste data from Excel into a Word document, a PowerPoint presentation or an Access database. When you copy and paste data into these applications the data is displayed in a table in the destination application.

You can also copy and paste charts from Excel into a Word document or a PowerPoint presentation.

## 12.3 Linking data

If you want the data that you copy into your file to be kept in line with the data held in Excel, you should create a link to it. You can use the Paste options or Copy and Paste Special to create a link.

**To link data:**

1 Start Excel *and* the application you want to copy data to.

2 Select the chart or data you want to copy.

3 Click the **Copy** tool 🔲 on the Standard toolbar.

4 Switch to the application you want to copy into.

5 Place the insertion point where you want the chart or data to appear.

6 Paste the data using the **Paste** tool.

7 Click the **Paste options** button.

8 Choose a link option.

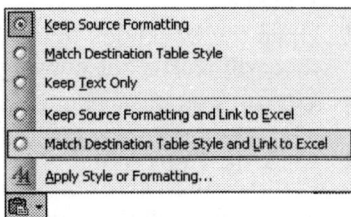

Or

9 Open the **Edit** menu and choose **Paste Special**.

10 Select the **Paste Link** button.

11 Choose an option from the **As:** list – when you select an option a brief description of how it works appears in the Result box.

12 Click **OK**.

When copied in this way, the chart or data displayed in the destination file is linked to the original data in Excel. Should you edit the data in the Excel worksheet, it will be updated automatically in your document or presentation.

# 12.4 Embedding data

You can copy and paste, or use Paste Special to get data or charts from Excel into a document in Word or PowerPoint. However, if you want data in Word or PowerPoint, and it isn't already set up in Excel (and doesn't need to be), you can insert a worksheet into a Word or PowerPoint file. It will be created and edited using Excel functions.

The Excel worksheet you insert will be an embedded object.

**To insert a Microsoft Excel worksheet:**

**1** Place the insertion point where you want the worksheet to appear in your Word document or PowerPoint presentation.

**2** Click the **Insert Microsoft Excel Worksheet** tool 📊 on the Standard toolbar.

**3** Click and drag over the grid to specify the worksheet size.

◆ You end up with an embedded worksheet, with the toolbars and menus of Excel displayed.

**4** Set up your worksheet as normal.

4 x 4 Spreadsheet

**5** Click anywhere outside the worksheet area when you've finished to return to your Word or PowerPoint file.

◆ To edit your worksheet, double-click on it – you will then be returned to Excel.

# 12.5 Mail Merge

Data in an Excel workbook can be used in a Mail Merge in Word. The workbook is used as the Data Document in the merge.

From the worksheets that have been set up in this book, the student results worksheet could be merged into a Word document so that we could send letters out to our students telling them how well they had done in their exams. You could add columns to contain the student address details to the worksheet.

**1** The top row of your data should contain the field names. Enter the data that will be merged into your document on the worksheet starting under the field name row.

**2** In Word, set up your Mail Merge document in the normal way. Select your Excel workbook when you open your DataSource.

**3** Choose the sheet required, or select the named range that contains the data you wish to use.

**4** Complete the Main Document in Word using the fields from your worksheet.

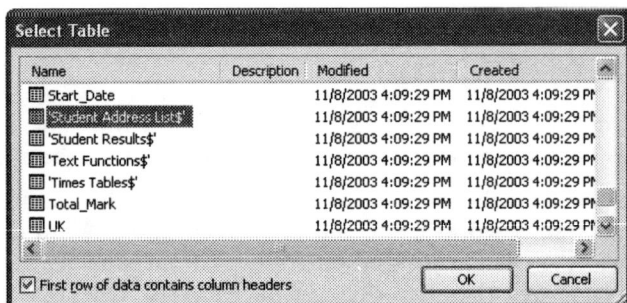

## Summary

In this chapter we have discussed:

* The difference between linking and embedding data

* Copy and Paste

* Linking the source data in an Excel workbook with the copy in Word or PowerPoint using *Copy and Paste Special*

* Embedding a worksheet in Word and in PowerPoint

* Merging an Excel list into a Word Mail Merge document

# 13

## excel and the web

**In this chapter you will learn**

- how to send your workbooks by e-mail
- about hyperlinks
- how to set up your data on Web pages

## Aims of this chapter

This chapter discusses using Excel with the wider world. You will learn how to e-mail an Excel workbook. You will also learn how to use hyperlinks to link to other files on your own computer or network, and to pages on the World Wide Web. Finally, we'll create a web document from within Excel and discuss how to publish it to the Web. The examples here are based on the use of Outlook Express for e-mail. You must also have access to the Internet, and be familiar with its basics, for this chapter.

# 13.1 E-mail

Provided you have a modem, communications software and a service provider, you can e-mail your Excel workbook to anywhere in the world. E-mail is usually very fast – sometimes your message will be delivered almost instantly, other times it may take an hour or so.

You can e-mail an open workbook directly from Excel. The whole workbook can be sent as a file 'attachment' to the message or the current worksheet can be sent, as text, as the body of the message – though this option is only available if Outlook or Outlook Express is your default e-mail application.

**To e-mail a workbook from within Excel:**

1 Open the workbook you want to e-mail.

2 Click the **E-mail** tool 🔲 .

3 Select the option required and click **OK**.

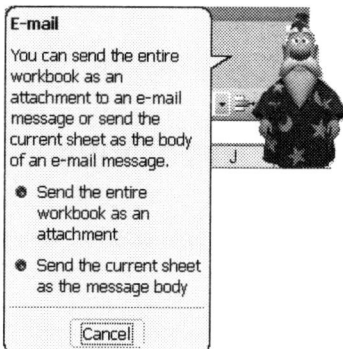

**E-mail**

You can send the entire workbook as an attachment to an e-mail message or send the current sheet as the body of an e-mail message.

- ⦿ Send the entire workbook as an attachment

- ⦿ Send the current sheet as the message body

[Cancel]

4 Enter the address you want to send the message to (or open the Address Book and select it from the list).

5 Enter or edit the subject as necessary.

6 Type in your message.

7   Click **Send** (if you opted to send the whole workbook) or **Send this sheet** (if you opted to send the current sheet).

**To attach a workbook from within your mail software:**

1   Click the **Create a New Mail Message** tool.

2   Enter the address in the **To:** field and **Cc:** field if necessary.

3   Type in your subject.

4   Key in your message.

5   Click the **Attach** tool [Attach].

6   Select the file you want to attach and click **Attach** in the **Open File** dialog box.

7   Repeat steps 5–6 if you want more than one file attached.

8   Send your message.

## 13.2 Hyperlinks

A hyperlink is a 'hot spot' that lets you jump from your workbook to another location – on your own computer, on your company network or anywhere in the world via the Internet.

## Adding hyperlinks

You can insert a hyperlink anywhere in your workbook. The text usually appears blue, with a blue underline, and when you click on it, the file that it points to will be displayed on screen.

### To insert a hyperlink to a file on your system:

1  Select the cell you want to place your hyperlink in.

2  Click the **Insert Hyperlink** tool 🔳 on the Standard toolbar.

3  Select **Existing File or Web Page** in the **Link to:** options.

4  Locate the file on your system.

5  Click **OK**.

### To insert a hyperlink to a place within the workbook:

1  Select the cell for the hyperlink and click 🔳.

2  Select **Place in This Document** in the **Link to:** options.

3  Use a cell address or a sheet name or named range in a workbook to specify the location required.

4  Select a sheet and enter the cell range required, or select the named range required from the **Defined Names** list.

5  Click **OK** to return to the **Worksheet** dialog box.

### To insert a hyperlink to a URL on the Web:

1  Select the cell for the hyperlink and click 🔳.

2  Select **Existing File or Web Page** in the **Link to:** options.

You can jump to a named place or a cell on a selected sheet in a workbook

**3** Type in the Address of the file you want to jump to.

Or

**4** Click [@] and browse the Web.

**5** Locate the page you want to link to.

**6** Return to Excel – click **Microsoft Excel** on the Task bar.

**7** Click **OK** at the **Insert Hyperlink** dialog box.

• You can edit the contents of the **Text to display** field to get a user-friendly prompt in a cell, rather than the full URL.

If you didn't enter a user-friendly prompt in the **Text to display** field when setting up your hyperlink (or if you want to change a URL) you can edit the hyperlink as necessary.

**To edit a hyperlink:**

1 Right-click on the cell that contains the hyperlink you wish to edit.

2 Select **Edit Hyperlink...** from the menu.

3 Edit the hyperlink details as required, e.g. enter the text you want to display in place of the URL in the **Text to display** field.

4 Click **OK**.

**To remove a hyperlink:**

1 Right-click on the cell that contains the hyperlink.

2 Select **Remove Link**.

| Cut |
| Copy |
| Paste |
| Paste Special... |
| Insert... |
| Delete... |
| Clear Contents |
| Insert Comment |
| Format Cells... |
| Pick From Drop-down List... |
| Add Watch |
| Create List... |
| Edit Hyperlink... |
| Open Hyperlink |
| Remove Hyperlink |
| Look Up... |

**Edit Hyperlink**

Text to display: karate

Link to: Existing File or Web Page / Place in This Document / Create New Document / E-mail Address

Look in: Excel 2003

Chapter 1, Chapter 10, Chapter 11, Chapter 12, Chapter 13, Chapter 2, Chapter 3, Chapter 4, Chapter 5, Chapter 6

Address: http://www.jkascotland.com/

ScreenTip... / Bookmark... / Remove Link / OK / Cancel

## Using hyperlinks

**To jump to a hyperlink location:**

• Point to the hyperlink – the mouse pointer becomes a hand with a pointing finger – and click.

When you jump to a file using a hyperlink, the **Web** toolbar is displayed.

If the toolbar doesn't appear, right-click on any toolbar and choose **Web** from the list.

Previous page   Go to Home page

Stop loading   Show only Web toolbar

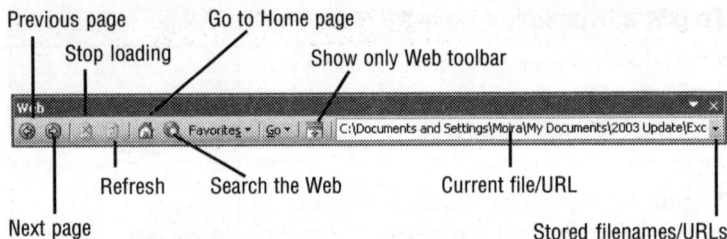

Refresh   Search the Web   Current file/URL

Next page

Stored filenames/URLs

- To return to the workbook you jumped from, click the Back button on the Web toolbar.

Once you've jumped to a hyperlink, then returned to your workbook, the hyperlink field changes colour – usually to violet. This will remind you that you've already used that hyperlink.

## 13.3 Preparing a web page

The pages you access through the Internet are part of the World Wide Web. You can create your own pages from Excel and publish them on the Web if you wish.

- To see how your workbook would look if you published it on the Web, open your workbook then choose **Web Page Preview** from the **File** menu.

Web pages published from Excel can be interactive or non-interactive. If the web page is to be viewed, but not manipulated by the viewer, don't make the web page interactive. If you want to allow users to interact with the data on your web page, e.g. sort or filter it, you can make the web page interactive. Both options are discussed below.

- Make sure you save your workbook as usual before you create a web page from any part of it. You can then go back to the original workbook if necessary.

To prepare a page for the Web you must save it in a web page file.

**To save a web page:**

1   Open the workbook you want to prepare for publication.

2   Choose **Save as Web Page...** from the **File** menu.

3   Specify the path and file name for your file.

| Order ID | Date | Customer | Town | Roses | Lilies | Carnations |
|---|---|---|---|---|---|---|
| FF100 | 01/12/2003 | Fabby Flowers | Edinburgh | 30 | 10 | 20 |
| GT001 | 03/12/2003 | Golden Tulip | Dalkeith | 20 | 20 | 40 |
| AF001 | 03/12/2003 | Amy's Flowers | Edinburgh | 50 | 60 | 80 |
| FF101 | 04/12/2003 | Fabby Flowers | Edinburgh | 22 | 10 | 50 |
| AF002 | 04/12/2003 | Amy's Flowers | Edinburgh | 60 | 30 | 20 |
| GT002 | 06/12/2003 | Golden Tulip | Dalkeith | 16 | 22 | 30 |
| BB001 | 06/12/2003 | Best Blooms | Dalkeith | 10 | 20 | 30 |
| GT003 | 07/12/2003 | Golden Tulip | Dalkeith | 20 | 18 | 30 |
| AF003 | 07/12/2003 | Amy's Flowers | Edinburgh | 60 | 50 | 90 |
| FF102 | 08/12/2003 | Fabby Flowers | Edinburgh | 16 | 20 | 30 |
| GT004 | 09/12/2002 | Golden Tulip | Dalkeith | 20 | 24 | 30 |
| FF103 | 10/12/2003 | Fabby Flowers | Edinburgh | 18 | 22 | 50 |
| BB002 | 10/12/2003 | Best Blooms | Dalkeith | 20 | 20 | 20 |
| GT005 | 11/12/2003 | Golden Tulip | Dalkeith | 14 | 20 | 70 |
| GT006 | 12/12/2002 | Golden Tulip | Dalkeith | 14 | 16 | 60 |
| FF104 | 15/12/2003 | Fabby Flowers | Edinburgh | 16 | 20 | 80 |
| BB003 | 15/12/2003 | Best Blooms | Dalkeith | 30 | 50 | 70 |
| GT006 | 16/12/2003 | Golden Tulip | Dalkeith | 20 | 30 | 50 |

**4** Click **Publish**.

**5** Select the data you wish to publish in the **Choose** field (or select *Range of Cells* and specify the range of cells).

**6** Select/deselect the **Add interactivity with** checkbox as required.

**7** If you wish to enter a **Title** at the top of your published page, click **Change**, enter the title you want to use in the **Set Title** dialog box and click **OK**.

**8** To preview the page, select the *Open published web page in browser* checkbox.

**9** Click **Publish**.

♦ A web file, e.g. Page.htm, will be saved in the location specified in the **File name** field and the page will appear on your screen.

A non-interactive page can be viewed on the Web, but not manipulated. An interactive Web page displays a toolbar that can be

A non-interactive Excel web page.

used to manipulate the data on the web page. You can sort, filter, copy and paste, etc. on an interactive page. Changes made to the page are not saved. Each time the page is accessed it will be displayed as it was originally set up.

◆ Close your web browser when you've finished viewing your page.

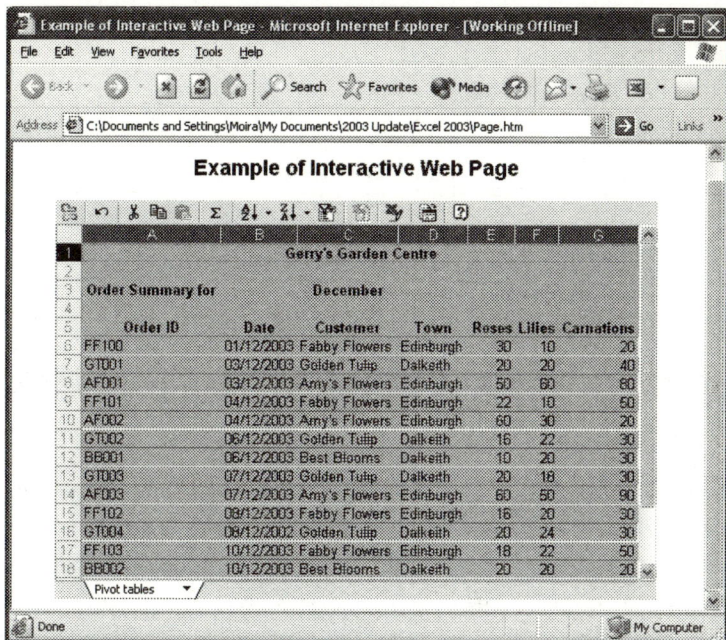

An interactive web page – note the tools available to the reader.

## 13.4 Editing your web page

You can easily update your web page as necessary.

**To update the workbook containing the data and the web page:**

1 Open the workbook.

2 Update as necessary.

3 Save the workbook.

4 Work through steps **2–9** on pages 202–203.

5 Chose **Replace File** at the prompt to replace an item that has already been published.

Microsoft Excel ✕

❓ The file 'C:\Documents and Settings\Moira\My Documents\2003 Update\Excel 2003\Page.htm' already exists. Do you want to replace the file, or add data to the existing file?

[ Replace file ]  [ Add to file ]  [ Cancel ]

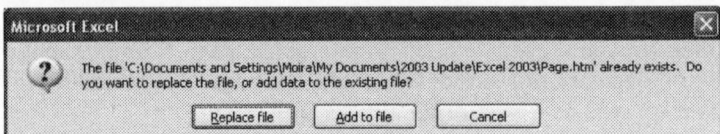

**To update a web page but not the workbook:**

1 Open the web page in Excel.

2 Edit as required.

3 Click **Save** and close the file.

• You can open a web page file in Excel or in your browser, from the Open dialog box. If you want to open the file in your browser to view it rather than edit it, click the Open button's drop-down arrow and choose **Open in Browser**.

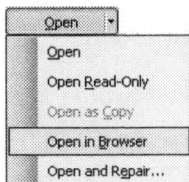

| Open ▾ |
| --- |
| Open |
| Open Read-Only |
| Open as Copy |
| Open in Browser |
| Open and Repair... |

## 13.5 Publishing to the Web

To publish your web page to the Web you must copy your file from your own computer to your service provider's server. This will be switched on 24 hours a day, so anyone who knows the URL of your web page will be able to access it at any time.

You may have folders set up in *My Network Places* (on the **Places** bar in the **Save As** dialog box) for your files, or you could publish them to MSN.

Most service providers will allocate some free storage space to you for your own web pages – 10 Mb (about 7 diskettes' worth) is fairly typical.

There are a number of ways to upload files to a web server – contact your service provider to find out how to upload to their server.

If you have created hyperlinks in your web page that jump to other files on your computer, remember to upload all the files, not just the main page.

To keep your files on the Web up to date, remember to update them and copy the new versions to your service provider's server as necessary.

# 13.6 Research

If you create worksheets where you need to research details, you may find the Research feature useful. This enables you to quickly reference information on your computer or online without leaving Excel. The research options include a thesaurus, translation tools and access to online references sites.

It's easy to use and you can customize its settings to suit your own research needs.

You can access Research from the bottom of the Search Results Task Pane or from the Standard toolbar.

**1** Click the **Research** tool 🔲 on the Standard toolbar.

**2** Type in the word or phrase you want to research.

**3** Choose your research places from the reference books and sites available.

**4** Click ➡.

The results of your search will be displayed in the Task Pane.

**5** Scroll through the Task Pane and read any suitable articles.

**To customize your research options by adding services to them:**

**1** Click **Get Services on Office Marketplace**.

**2** Explore the services available.

**3** Copy the web address of the service you require.

**4** Go back to Excel.

**5** Click **Research Options...** at the bottom of the Research Task Pane.

**Research** ▾ ✕

Search for:

investment opportunities

Gale Company Profiles

Back

**Gale Company Profiles (1–5 of 19)**

Next

Brought to you by THOMSON GALE

**J.P. Morgan Partners (BHCA), L.P.**

**Address** 1221 Ave. of the Americas
New York, NY 10020

**Email** contactus@jpmorganpartners.c

**Phone** 212-899-3400

**Fax** 212-899-3401

**Web** http://www.jpmorganpartners.c

**Firm Type** Private Subsidiary, Headqu

**Revenue** $30,000,000,000.00

**Employees** 150

**Revenue Per Employee** $200,000,0

**Fiscal Year End** 12/31/2002

**Year Founded** 1984

**Primary SIC** 6799 Investors, Not Else

View Complete Profile...

Get services on Office Marketplace

Research options...

**Research Options**

To activate a service for searching, select the check box associated with that service.

Services:

**Reference Books**
- [ ] Encarta Dictionary: English (North America)
- [x] Encarta Dictionary: English (U.K.)
- [ ] Encarta Dictionary: French
- [ ] Thesaurus: English (Australia)
- [x] Thesaurus: English (Canada)
- [x] Thesaurus: English (U.K.)
- [ ] Thesaurus: English (U.S.)
- [ ] Thesaurus: French (Canada)
- [ ] Thesaurus: French (France)
- [ ] Thesaurus: Spanish (Spain-Modern Sort)
- [x] Translation

**Research Sites**
- [x] eLibrary
- [ ] Encarta Encyclopedia: English (North America)

Properties...

[ Add Services... ] [ Update/Remove... ] [ Parental Control... ]

[ OK ] [ Cancel ]

6 Choose **Add Services...**

7 Paste the address into the **Address** box.

8 Click **Add**.

---

## Summary

In this final chapter we have covered how to:

- Send and receive e-mail messages

- Create hyperlinks to other files, to places in a workbook and to web pages

- Display a user-friendly prompt for hyperlinks

- Create interactive and non-interactive pages for publication to the Web

- Edit web files

- Find out about publishing your web pages

- Search the Internet or your network from within Excel

**taking it further**

If you've mastered half of what's in this book, you are well on the way to becoming a proficient Excel user. If you are getting to grips with most of it, you are doing very well indeed.

You'll find lots of information on Excel on the Internet, in addition to the **Help** menu option Microsoft Office Online that takes you to http://office.microsoft.com/home/default.aspx

You could also try searching the Web for sites that provide information on Excel. Try entering "Microsoft Excel" + "Software Reviews" into your search engine. You should come up with several sites worth a look.

If you would like to join a course to consolidate your skills, you could try your local college, or search the Internet for on-line courses. Most courses cost money, but you may find the odd free one – try searching for *+Excel +Tutorial +Free*.

Good Excel skills are useful on many levels – personal, educational and vocational. Now that you have improved your Excel skills, why not consider going for certification? The challenge of an exam can be fun, and a recognized certificate may improve your job prospects. There are a number of different bodies that you could consider.

You may want to consider Microsoft Office Specialist exams or ECDL (European Computer Driving Licence – basic or advanced) certification. Or, if you feel more ambitious, how about other Microsoft Certified Professional exams!

Visit **http://www.microsoft.com/learning/mcp/officespecialist/ requirements.asp** for information on MOS certification or **http://www.ecdl.com** for information on ECDL.

# index